Book of Jewels

for personal development

by

Craig Stewart

Book of Jewels
for personal development
Copyright © 2020 Craig Stewart
All Rights Reserved

ISBN-13:978-0-578-59504-7

Published by Craig Stewart
Impeccable Works, LLC
www.CraigTheWriterStewart.com

Cover Design By: BOSS Branding, LLC - BossBrandingllc.com

LEGAL DISCLAIMER

This book is a work of Creative Non-Fiction. No names have been changed, no characters have been invented, no events fabricated. It reflects the author's present recollection of experiences over time. Some names have been omitted, some events have been compressed, and some dialogue has been recreated.

Also by Craig Stewart:

Words Never Spoken: A Memoir
One Thing for Certain, Two Things for Sure: A Memoir Continued…
and
So Much To Say, a Book of Quotes

DEDICATION

A Love Letter to Black People

"You are the descendant of slaves that would not quit." Susan L. Taylor, former Editor in Chief of Essence magazine, spoke those words at Hampton University when I was an undergraduate. She continued by saying, "There isn't anything that you can't do. You are here because they would not die."

In the past when I considered giving up in business or as a writer, because the road became difficult at times, I'd think about them, my people, and her words. I reminded myself that I could never give up because they couldn't, and because I have their blood running through my veins. I do it for them. I rely on their strength. It helps motivate me when I want to quit. I keep going because of them.

Our strength as a people is recorded in history and it is unmatched. I love everything there is about being Black—our prevailing strength, resilience, adaptability, the rhythm with which we move and speak, our natural instinct to overcome, re-create and survive.

Our predecessors understand our potential in ways that some of us have yet to learn. It's the reason the playing field has always been uneven, and why the finish line is constantly moving. They know that if the playing field ever became level that we would be unstoppable. Moreover, they fear that we would do to them what they've done to us.

I'd be remiss if I didn't say that I didn't always love everything about us as a people. I'm guilty of being harder, more judgmental of us than I should've been in the past. I was embarrassed by the ills of the community—the "ghetto" language which some of us use to speak, the rising number of underage single mothers, deadbeat fathers, the inflated prison and addiction rates, the failing school systems—until I realized a few things.

One, the media wanted Black people to see and believe these things about other Black people, even though these things weren't completely true. Two, it was my own concern about how White people saw and thought of us—until I divorced myself from those thoughts and any concern about the White gaze. Finally, I realized that we've been severely marginalized by a system designed to encourage us to fail because our potential is limitless.

Despite all that we've been through, we survive with dignity while managing to produce greatness. We've managed to find some joy in our hardest moments in this country because we're magic. The world knows it. Many hate us because of it. We remain the envy of the world for our brilliance and genius. Thus, it's important to me that I use my gift to help re-write the narrative of the Black experience in this country without exception. In other words, it's important that I tell as much of our truth as possible, including the stuff we don't enjoy hearing about ourselves because it's uncomfortable. It's my job as an artist, because I see myself as more than a writer.

It isn't my intention to divide us or incite hate. My idea is to provoke you and anyone that comes into contact with my art to see things from a different perspective. Whether it's my podcast, *So Much to Say*, my books, or my stage plays, I want you to walk away from the experience feeling and thinking differently.

As I write this dedication, this love letter to Black people, I realize that these words are like a dog whistle, sure to incite curiosity from anyone who isn't Black; questioning whether or not racism is at play here. The idea that I must despise White people because I love Black people is absurd. It's crazy to think that racism is at play because I say out loud that I love Black people, and if reading those words translates as White hate for you, then White privilege and Whiteness are to blame for trying to rob me of my sense of pride, and trying to colonize my Blackness.

It's not enough for me to say, "I'm not racist," because statements like that require proof that can only be verified through actions. The same is true when White people say, "I don't see color," or "Some of my closest friends are Black," yet, some demonstrate biases based on race because color is the first thing we see. So, to answer simply, because I'm for my people doesn't mean I'm against anyone else.

I just love Black people and all that we've managed to accomplish with the scraps left behind for us, with which we've managed to make something out of nothing. I'm charged with the responsibility of being sweeter and kinder to, and more supportive of people of color because we've been excluded from so much—we deserve that from each other at the very least. I'm ready to see us win in a major way because we haven't enjoyed the luxury or stability of intergenerational wealth at a scale equal to that of White folks.

I'm really clear, like most Black people, that shit isn't going well for us in this country and it's been going wrong for quite some time. I think it's safe to say that many of us are disturbed by very specific systems of racism: gentrification, the prison system, the disparities in education, and within politics, to name a few. It would require too much from me to dismantle each of these systems, but I will say if you haven't already seen the documentary *13th - From*

Slave to Freedom on Netflix, then please do so. It's a really great start to understand the Black experience in the United States. It does a beautiful job of showing how the prison system in this country is really an extension of slavery in a modern form.

The disadvantages and disparities that we face as a people are evidenced in the news, television programming, and award shows that purport to promote excellence, but somehow manage to exclude Black and Brown people systematically. White skin doesn't influence what White people feel when they see unarmed Black people being shot down in the streets by cops—their life experiences do. White people who recognize these injustices aren't offended by these truths because they are equally outraged, and honest enough with themselves to acknowledge that there's a problem in this country between the police and criminal justice systems and communities of color.

This book is dedicated to the memory of Trayvon Benjamin Martin. I'll remember forever where I was, and everything I felt when the verdict was announced. I had no words. Anger and melancholy left me speechless. A day later, I was challenged to create more purposeful work that provokes change and illuminates evil, hate and fear similar to that which snuffed a light so bright. A hero emerged that night. You, Trayvon. You forced us all to take a closer look at ourselves individually, as a community and as a people. Your life mattered. These words are for you. Recorded forever in history. Gone but never forgotten.

These names have been etched in our hearts & minds, recorded in history, never to be forgotten: Amadou Diallo, Sean Bell, Oscar Grant, Rekia Boyd, Trayvon Martin, Michael Brown, Eric Garner, Tamir Rice, Laquan McDonald, Philando Castile, Freddie Gray, Sandra Bland, Alton Sterling, and many others.

CONTENTS

ACKNOWLEDGEMENTS

To my mother, Gladys Stewart, thank you for loving me through it all. You were first to believe and support my dream to write. Initially, you thought writing was just a hobby that I could do on the side, until you witnessed my first stage play sell out. Thank you for seeing the end goal and whispering encouraging words when I got discouraged along the way. I love you more than I say.

To my father, Milton Stewart Jr., thank you for telling me as a little boy, "I'm proud of you," and, "You can do anything you put your mind to because you're smart." I believed it, so I did it. I love you.

I'm grateful for friends who encouraged me to dream when it became difficult to dream. I'd be remiss if I didn't single out Thaddeus Lancaster and Torrance Smith. Thank you both for all you've done silently to help push my dream forward. I'm equally thankful for the kindness of strangers who support my work because they're inspired by the work, or simply because they wish to celebrate my effort. Thank you for believing and trusting my gift.

And to my online family, the Penpals on Facebook and YouTube, I love you equally. You've pushed me as much as you say I've encouraged you. Thank you for lifting me from very desperate times and being so consistent in your support. It's one thing to have social media followers; it's another to have social media supporters. There are social media influencers with hundreds of thousands of followers but they lack the level of support you've shown me. This book, this success belongs to you as much as it belongs to me. You invested in me. You invested in my dream. You stayed up late to watch my online foolishness and smart talk. You missed me whenever I didn't show up online and made it your business to let me know that my absence wasn't appreciated. You cried with me. You laughed with me. You laughed at me. But, most importantly we learned from each other and we grew together. I love you for loving me and allowing me the privilege to do what I love…create! Today truly is a good day for thinkers, thought-leaders, progressives and dreamers around the world.

FOREWORD

Communication. Who are we without the exchange of words or actions that allow us to tell our stories, share our thoughts, express our fears and profess our love? Long before 1619, before our people were torn from the continent of Africa, we were a people of varied means of expression, connection and communication. We had tribal dialects and languages, piercings, proud scars, hairstyles and garb that spoke to and for us.

When we arrived at our new habitat, which included parts of the Caribbean, America, and other parts of the world, we were stripped of our history, our culture, our familiar neighbors, and we were forced to connect with newness. Obvious differences of skin color kept us apart from others, yet closest to each other. We learned to communicate. Words. A song. A story. A quote. Each had a meaning...exact or left open for interpretation.

Craig Stewart is rooted in and grounded by words. He is a lover of communication, connection and expression. It's why we became fast friends while attending Hampton University. As a man of service who is committed to all of our people being seen, heard and celebrated, Craig depends on the impact of words, the weight of sentence structure and the meaning of a phrase to deliver emotions, ignite passions and inspire new thoughts and evolution.

Life is a blessing. The ability to feel is a gift. To live a life filled with feelings, reflections, lessons, defeats and victories is honor. Craig Stewart has lived! Experience is the best teacher and Craig took notes. His decision to share his life and love with the world is evident in his writing. Sometimes the lesson is there for you to uncover along the journey of the story being told...in his play, his memoirs, or during one of his podcast episodes. In this book, Craig is standing at the front of the class, chalk in hand, graciously sharing, educating and providing us with gems that you will indeed find helpful, and dare I say necessary, for a life rich with understanding, love and growth...should we all not continue to grow and live? ...until we die.

Danielle M. Brown
Founder, The Heart To Say It
Cohost, Cocktails & Cancer Podcast

1 Life

You'll never have it all figured out—believe, trust, and know...

Craig Stewart

Several years ago, I considered giving up. Not on life, but on the dream of being a full-time writer and artist. I was anxious, losing faith and becoming quite weary. I didn't trust that things would level out for me. I was burning the candle at both ends of the stick yet again—still not realizing at that point that everything happens when and as it should. I was still trying to force the current and manipulate the process by expediting things. I tried to encourage success, while becoming frustrated along the way.

I was touring with two books, which meant juggling all the tour expenses: printing and shipping costs, travel from city to city either by car or plane, hotel stays coupled with eating out while on the road, all while trying to budget my personal living expenses back home. I was adept at surviving on very little. I could stretch pennies, but I was mentally exhausted from having to be resourceful and finding new ways to rob Peter to pay Paul. There never seemed to be enough money left over for me to relax and simply catch my breath.

At times it felt like I was drowning—suffocating even. I was doing the work that I had been called to do, but my finances were bleak. It didn't feel like I was moving forward. I knew what I was capable of and what was possible, but I wondered if I'd ever get there. I also knew what God was capable of doing but wondered if He would ever do it for me. Would my family and friends truly understand what I was going through, what I was trying to accomplish? I craved success—that proverbial place that we all imagine it to be.

At times, I thought I was going to lose my mind because it felt like the weight of the world was on my shoulders. I pined over things that were out of my control in a race to success. I felt a mental anguish that propelled me into this sort of internal battle with myself. My depression was brought on by trying to force the current. I tried to manipulate success. But I couldn't. Once I figured that out, and I released the reins to life, I was better off, and things began to happen. But until then, I suffered through many dark years of extreme sadness—a functional depression—because my faith was broken. This only amplified the fear and doubt that resided within.

I've felt depression. I came through it. My depression was more broken faith than anything, and it was steered by doubt. Depression interrupts our connection to a higher power. It distorts our reality and leads us to believe things are more dire than they are. The more I prayed the more difficult the way seemed.

My prayer was simple:

"Continue to bless me indeed, cover me, guide me and make me whole. Use my work, use my gifts to reach, teach and heal. Secure me. Protect me. Provide for me. Keep your hands upon me so that I do not cause evil or pain. Thank you for trusting me with this gift. Thank you for the ability to reason and make sound decisions. Thank you for good judgment. Thank you for keeping me safe, thank you for keeping me from sickness, harm, disease, disaster and tragedy. In Jesus' name I pray, amen."

I had already taken the leap. I just hadn't anticipated the bumps, bruises or scrapes that would come along the way, and throughout the fall. The mental anguish that I experienced was caused by a lack of trust that God would provide for me from day to day while chasing the dream, so I panicked. I prayed and then became more frustrated. But prayer isn't magic. Prayer allows us to connect with God, a source, to make the life we've been given manageable.

I didn't trust that I would be sustained through the process. What was missing was faith—the belief that I would be okay no matter what happened. Faith isn't always logical. It's a muscle, a spiritual muscle, that has to be exercised to prove effective. Someone reading these words is at that exact same point today that I was, and it's important that you know, giving up is not an option.

What if this time next year you'll be right where you dream of being? I can't promise you that, but what if? Think about it. Hope is more than enough to get you there. I know from experience that the life I once prayed for is the life I'm living now because I kept moving, I kept trusting and I never stopped believing.

I thought I had an unshakeable confidence that I would succeed, but somehow, I lost some of that confidence along the journey. I've often wondered, what changed? What triggered that doubt? What activated my fear? What caused me to be afraid to reach and risk? It wasn't one thing in particular that happened in a single moment. Rather, it happened over the course of time after a series of setbacks and let downs—after being bruised along the way. I tried tracing back to the point in my life where things shifted—the moment when I first began doubting myself, and all that I once believed to be possible. I began retracing my steps.

When I was in elementary school, I participated in an ongoing study conducted by Johns Hopkins University in Baltimore. The Johns Hopkins Beginning school studies program followed me, and hundreds of other elementary school students, from the beginning of our education through college. The last session I recall was over the phone, and it happened during my sophomore year at Hampton University.

But, twice a year—fall and spring—until my senior year in high school, I met face to face with someone from the program who asked a series of questions related to socialization at school and home, academic performance, family dynamics, and interpersonal behaviors and patterns. The purpose of the study was to isolate factors attributed to making some children successful in school, and why they continued on to be productive adults. It was also designed to determine the factors that pointed to reasons other children languish. A portion of the study centered on home routines that represented positive reinforcements, or those that had a potentially negative effect on a child's academic performance, as well as his or her ability to commingle with other students and teachers.

The administrator came prepared with test booklets containing hundreds of questions, and scantron sheets to fill in the bubbles as I gave answers for each. The sessions were in the middle of the school day, and at times they lasted well over an hour. I'm not certain how the other students were selected or even how I was selected to participate in the program, but I looked forward to the meetings because it meant that I had special permission to skip classes.

There was a wide range of questions such as:

- Is there an adult at home when you arrive from school or do you use a key to let yourself in;

- Do both of your parents live in the home with you;

- Is there a parent assisting you with homework or are you responsible for doing it alone;

- Do your parent(s) check to see if you've completed your homework;

- Are there chores that you're responsible for completing at home;

- Do you typically watch television when you get home or are you required to complete your homework assignments first;

- What kind of grades do you receive;

- And a host of other questions that were a bit more involved.

I was fortunate to have parents who were hands on. Although I was a latchkey kid, my mother assisted me with completing my homework assignments until I was responsible enough to do it alone. But even then, she asked about my assignments to make sure I had them completed, and I was well into high school by that time.

My mother was never a stranger at parent-teacher conferences either. I was also involved in a string of extracurricular activities that she enrolled me in, such as art classes, little league baseball, karate, swimming, and ice-skating lessons.

The Johns Hopkins Beginning school studies program was one of the seminal indicators to foreshadow the quintessence of my life, but there were other clues also. In fact, there were clues threaded throughout my childhood that pointed to greater purpose on the horizon.

One of my elementary school English teachers allowed me to proctor her spelling tests a time or two when she needed to step away from the classroom, which had been unheard of previously. It wasn't just that I had perfect scores on my spelling tests. She saw something in me.

Then there were countless neighbors, family, peers, and strangers who saw something different about me.

"There's something about your aura," they all said.

Intrinsically, I felt it too, but I had no idea they could see it.

At the time I couldn't articulate how this sort of knowledge about my life's work would affect people—some whom I would know, and many I would not.

I often said to my mother, "I'm gonna be rich one day," because as a child that was the only way I could articulate this internal feeling. I distinctly remember my mother saying, "Stop dreaming so big." I never understood this because it's the opposite of what we should tell our children.

Years later in college a friend quizzed, "What if it never happens for you? Have you thought about what you'll do? Would you be devastated?" She smirked and waited eagerly for my response.

She was referring to success, financial success, but on some level, I knew I would connect to my passion, my purpose and follow it no matter how difficult it became. This passion had nothing to do with money at all. Moreover, I had never thought about *it* not happening. In fact, I never considered a plan B per se, until years later when life happened and seemed to disrupt things.

After college I found myself on a path completely unrelated to the course that I wanted my life to take. I thought by the time I was 25 years old that I'd be a millionaire. I kept this belief until I reached 24 and had no choice but to push my lofty goal to 30. Still, at 30 I wasn't a millionaire, and no one could've convinced me that at the very least I wouldn't have owned a home by the time I was 35 years old.

But by 35, after relocating to Los Angeles, I was living in the homes of various friends because I couldn't afford a place of my own. I made up some fake pay stubs to purchase a car that my father would co-sign for me to get. It was a painful truth that I hated to admit to myself. That realization was one of the first to shake my confidence. It seemed I had wandered completely off course. It felt like I was failing, but I was failing forward, and didn't realize it at the time. Even when it feels like you're off course, you're still on course because everything has purpose in the grand scheme of things—including the detours and setbacks. Those detours caused a shift in how I approached my ambition. If you see them as such, setbacks are turning points. I became more cautious, but those setbacks gave me new opportunities to step up and start again.

I wasn't displaced because of poor planning or anything I had done wrong. Rather, it was just my station in life at the time, but it was exactly where I needed to be. I seemed to be veering off course, and the distractions caused me to think it would never happen; thus some of my ambition was replaced with doubt. Once doubt slinks in, its only job is to convince us that the possible is impossible—that we aren't enough.

I began questioning whether or not writing was what I was called to do, because I found myself working jobs that I would never have considered previously, and I felt so far away from my dream. I wasn't employed at those places because I wanted to be—dire financial circumstances caused me to be. Regardless, there were omens at each of those jobs that suggested something greater was ahead of me.

I remember working as a host at a neighborhood restaurant in Atlanta. My main responsibility at the restaurant was seating guests and answering the phone to book reservations. I couldn't help but think about what needed to happen in order for me to be free of what seemed to be pointless work at a menial job. I spent many afternoons daydreaming about a career as a full-time writer that would afford me the luxury of making a living with my craft.

When I accepted the job at the restaurant, I didn't have a car to get to or from work. Nevertheless, I managed to get there every day without relying on public transportation. My friend Willie called or texted me every morning, before I had a chance to worry, to see if I had a way to and from work. I began to trust the process called life just a bit, but I needed further evidence that it was ok to trust the universe again, and little by little, I began to receive new clues.

There was a woman dining alone in the restaurant one evening who caught my attention. I noticed her noticing me as I passed by her table to seat other guests. When I looked her way again, she beckoned for me to come over to her table.

"What's your name?" she said with a heavy southern accent.

"Craig," I said with a smile.

"What do you do?" she asked squinting as if she was trying to figure me out. It was as if she knew something about me that I hadn't told her, and she was quizzing me to see if I would come clean with the truth.

"I'm the host," I replied.

"No, I mean, what else do you do? This isn't all that you do," she said pointing her finger around the restaurant.

"I'm a writer," I beamed.

She looked at me quizzically. Halfway squinting her eyes.

"Have a seat," she said tapping the seat of the booth. "I knew this wasn't the only thing you did. You don't belong here," she said confidently.

Without fail, God left little clues, omens, small glimmers of light on the road to light my path when it was too dark for me to see, and those clues usually came from perfect strangers.

That moment solidified that God is always speaking, although we're not always listening. God speaks to us through people, and I believe He was using that woman that day in the restaurant to remind me of my purpose. But it wasn't the first time He had sent a reminder to me along my journey.

Earlier that same evening, two other patrons mistook me for the restaurant manager. Subsequently, two of the managers pulled me to the side. First, they offered compliments on the black dinner jacket that I wore to work that day. Then they asked me not to wear it to work again to avoid confusion in the future.

At the time, I thought it was the jacket that caused the problem, but it wasn't the jacket. It was my energy—that thing called aura that I heard so much about as a kid. That incident was another simple reminder that I could've easily overlooked. Plenty of times in previous years I had overlooked signs because I wasn't paying close enough attention to my life. But this time I heard Him in a different way—with fresh ears. God was speaking again. Even when your life feels like it's off course, people can still see the calling on your life.

That restaurant job was one of the many pit stops I would make along the way that offered a bounty of life lessons that I'd need—that I couldn't have gotten anyplace else. There were times it felt as if I had abandoned my passion because personal storms in my life required all my attention, and those demands couldn't wait. I accepted many jobs that seemingly had nothing to do with my career, and sometimes those jobs lasted a year or more. I thought they were in the way of my career. It became difficult at times trying to decipher whether I was being patient on the journey or becoming complacent because of a lack of progress. But I was exactly where I needed to be for the lessons that I needed to get. There was something for me at every one of those jobs despite how insignificant I thought they were at the time.

Circumstances can never prevent what's already in motion—what's meant to be, what's destined to happen. I was right where I needed to be because it was all by design—every single obstacle.

We could allow those obstacles that we stumble over along the way to permanently distract us. Or we could simply make the decision to jump over them or go around them, then move towards the possibilities despite the scrapes on our knees. Even the setbacks are a part of the fabric of our story. We may not choose certain situations, jobs or circumstances for our life, but fate merges with destiny to create such experiences and relationships to offer us lessons we would otherwise miss. The road ahead must have twists and turns; otherwise we would run straight for the goal without making any detours, which ultimately would cause us to bypass life's biggest lessons as well as the wisdom that God gifts us along the way.

We need those lessons to gain knowledge that will undoubtedly grow us exponentially. Life happens and will continue to happen. We have to adapt to whatever comes. The things we resist cause us the most stress. We have to be willing to move wherever the wind blows us. It may feel as if the forces in the universe are holding us back, but there's purpose in it all. It's your responsibility to find purpose in everything.

Live confidently, knowing that the wait is always worth it. Trust that the end is still the end and everything on your journey has purpose and is designed to propel you forward the quickest and most efficient way possible.

At one of the lowest points in my life one of my mother's closest friends asked my mother if she felt that she had wasted her money sending me to college, because my Mom was still supporting me years after I had graduated from college. Her intention wasn't for it to get back to me or to hurt my feelings, but my ego was still bruised, nevertheless.

My mom replied optimistically. She explained that she had no regrets about supporting me, and that she only had hope that things would one day turn around for me. As an entrepreneur, my mother understood the discipline required to see a dream actualize, so she often encouraged me to continue writing, and to continue harvesting my dream, even though she knew I was mentally exhausted, losing faith and scraping pieces together day by day in desperation to survive.

My mother's friend had given power to an insecurity that I tried to shield with explanations over the years about why things hadn't quite materialized for me professionally. She had given voice to what I always believed people were secretly saying and thinking about me all along. How arrogant of me to think that everyone around me was busy watching, judging and waiting to see if I'd fail. These were life lessons for me. They were teachable moments. Besides, it's always easier for those who haven't lived your life to judge your life.

While most of the people I knew around my age were well into their careers, I seemed to be floundering. I was comparing the best of myself to other people. But my life had simply taken a different course. I failed to realize that my journey is my journey and no one else's.

Sure, I could have secured a corporate job with a great salary because I had a degree in journalism from Hampton University. But I'd decided against playing it safe as many do. Instead I chose to pursue my passion.

I remember working for the Coca-Cola Company just after college and watching hundreds of employees passing me by in the courtyard. I was unhappy there but had confidence that I wasn't the only person working for the company who had similar feelings about doing something else with their life and time on earth.

But, unlike many of those people who felt trapped by mortgages, kids in college and other responsibilities, I felt the freedom to walk away because I wasn't tied down by those things, so I could respond to my calling. I trusted my instincts. Instincts aren't taught. A child can sense that a growling dog is unapproachable without a warning from an adult. She knows instinctively not to get too close because she pays attention to all of the clues that the dog gives. But as we grow and begin to move through the world, we fail to listen to our instincts because we begin listening to and trusting the people closest to us more than we rely on our own gut. We forget how to read the warnings, or we ignore that intuitive nature.

I was working jobs that I resented rather than pursuing my passion. I hated going to work every morning, week after week, month after month, year after year knowing it wasn't a place I could work until retirement, all while wondering what could've happened had I possessed the courage to leave that job to follow my heart.

The twists and turns along the meandering career path I traveled were required, but grueling nonetheless. My credit was in ruins because I consistently paid my bills late or not at all, and I had invested most of what I'd earned from day jobs to produce a stage play and build a fledgling greeting card business. My credit cards were maxed out and my bank accounts were exhausted—some had even been closed by the banks because they were severely overdrawn.

At one point, I couldn't even open a bank account because I'd been reported to check systems for leaving a bank account overdrawn. But, for every single step that we take for ourselves, God takes three for us—even when we fail to acknowledge it.

During the last few years that I lived in Atlanta, I lived with a friend, and I could never escape feeling like I was invading her space. Most days I left the house before she returned from work. I wanted to give her an opportunity to come home to an empty home so she could unwind.

Initially, I thought I was the only beneficiary of her act of kindness, but I was only looking at the surface. In the greater context, the relationship was mutually beneficial. I brought something to her life as well. I learned to be more compassionate through her example of selflessness in allowing me to stay rent free, and I was filling a void for her because she was lonely and still healing from a breakup. It was all by design in the spiritual realm. It was the purest example of God knowing, with His infinite wisdom, what I needed, what she needed, and how we could serve each other through that arrangement.

My purpose for living with my friend transcended the most obvious reasons. I moved in because I needed a place to stay, and had to learn a bit more humility, but in turn she needed emotional support because she was suffering in ways that weren't financial. God knew that I was emotionally strong in ways that she was weak.

For a long time, I felt indebted to her because she fed, sheltered and gave me money at times, but l remembered that I had been that kind of friend to others at one time or another. I'd opened my home to other friends on two separate occasions because they found themselves displaced. This was the law of reciprocity at play, which works like a boomerang. Whatever you put out has to come back to you in one form or another. And that law is true even if it doesn't come back from the person that you blessed or hurt.

But, at the time, it was a bit unsettling for me to find myself in a predicament that would require me to live under someone else's roof and rules. It brought up feelings of inadequacy, insecurity, and moments of weakness that fed deep-seated feelings that created self-doubt. And, fear that I would never be financially independent.

Certainly, this was another one of those points in my life that shook my confidence and ultimately caused me to doubt myself more, because some way, somehow, my self-worth was attached to financial wellness. However, moments of weakness don't make us weak, they make us human. Moreover, friendship is sacred, and that time in my life reminded me that friendship is a responsibility. It isn't always convenient nor is it always reciprocal, but there should be balance.

It was a combination of all of these circumstances that I found myself in that caused me to pause and second-guess my potential. I do, however, remember the exact moment that I decided to rid myself of self-doubt. That moment occurred onboard a flight to Los Angeles in April 2011 when I relocated.

There is no exact answer for when or how your dream will manifest—whatever that dream is for you. Whether it's love, marriage, children or career, I will say, when you believe enough and take consistent action towards the dream, it shall come to pass. It has no other choice but to happen. With that, it's important to understand that the things we chase often elude us, so leave room for the universe to do its part. Don't stop living because you're chasing the dream and waiting for the dream to manifest. Keep living and experiencing life along the way. I used to punish myself when things weren't going well.

Life is beyond abundant if we choose to see it that way. Life is bountiful, despite what we think we lack. There are blessings in every single day. It's up to us to notice them.

God is gracious. He's merciful and faithful when you believe. It's a matter of perspective. When you begin to trust Him, things move into focus and align. Each day wake up hopeful…thankful. The more I attempt to understand the mechanics of life, the more I begin to see clearly how the universe conspires to work for my benefit.

I've wondered before why some are stricken with diseases or disabilities, but God knows what each of us needs to grow, how to get our attention, and bring us to our full potential. For me, learning came about because of financial difficulties, while others are pruned through divorce, becoming teenage parents, or through the death of a child or parent. He knows what each of us needs to develop us.

We often complicate things that could be simple. We muddle things that are already clear and make things harder for ourselves than they have to be because of the choices we make.

I panic less about things that I have no control over. I'm more settled when I'm facing a crisis because of past experiences. There's a rhythm to life, and once you've lived long enough, you learn to identify the signs because they start to feel familiar.

For me, it's like a light switch is flipped on inside. I can imagine myself on the other side of the crisis. Going in, I may not know how the resolution will come, but instinctively I know things will settle, as they should, as they always have. I manage to relax in the face of calamity because it feels familiar in ways. On some level deep down inside, I know that I'll be okay on the other side of whatever it is.

It is peace of mind, part wisdom, and the skill of surrendering to whatever comes—it's adapting. I also ask myself, "If today was the last day of my life, would any of this matter?" Thus far, the answer to that question has always been an emphatic no.

Those omens that I spoke of earlier in this chapter also serve to point us to the next best steps to take. There are markers in life that point to what's to come for you and me. In the book *The Alchemist*, the author Paulo Coelho refers to these foreshadowed events as omens. They point out opportunities and challenges on the horizon.

Think of the many puzzle pieces that your life is comprised of and how each fit together. Think of how each piece played an integral part in the events that make up your life—a breakup, sickness, someone's death, a termination or layoff, a move whether it was forced or voluntary. Each had a purpose that acted as a bridge for you to the people, opportunities and wisdom that you have today. Every circumstance played a part in who you've become.

Some would say your life is already decided—that it's fate. I'd say fate meets destiny at the intersection of choice.

Life is about choices, so live with intention. Live with purpose, even after life happens to you.

2 Dating

We all deserve love without suffering first...

Craig Stewart

We Are All Broken

We are all broken in some way, just broken in different places. We all have scars. We show up to our relationships with them. We bring the sum of our life experiences to every relationship or situationship—those encounters that never quite graduate to relationship status.

We're influenced by every person that's touched our life negatively or positively, every relationship that was modeled for us as children, every relationship that we've heard stories about, and every relationship that we've participated in. All of those experiences help shape what we think, feel and believe about love and relationships. They all help to inform who we are today.

We all have power. We're born with it. Some of you understand what I'm talking about. Others of you have yet to learn your power, but in time will grow into them. Many others may never understand their power. Looking back, I realize that I've been in relationships with men who hadn't learned their power, so they felt threatened by mine.

All of the qualities that drew them to me, made them insecure down the line once they were with me. My attributes were intimidating. My strength was like kryptonite to them. Some were in a secret competition with me without me knowing. They didn't want a partner. They didn't want their equal. They wanted someone they could intimidate. They wanted to be smarter. They wanted to be more successful. They were more concerned with being right in every argument. They wanted to win. They wanted someone they could control.

But those experiences aren't unique to me. I can think of five of my female friends who are well educated, own their home, who do not have children, and they make upwards of six figures. Yet, they're single, with no prospect in sight, because some men feel threatened by a partner that they can't control with money. These women are self-sufficient and financially independent. They're a catch, but they're also a threat to weak hearted, often insecure, men. Some men want partners that need them for survival, a partner who makes their ego comfortable. These women aren't those type of women.

I've noticed another trend with some Black men who recognize that they are a commodity in the dating pool because they stand out. They're highly educated, successful, professional, and have yet to father children. Now, this isn't an exact science, but oftentimes they take full advantage of their position and will opt to play the field for as long as they can because they know they are rare in many ways, and because they know they can.

I've met and dated some really broken men, and I too, was once severely broken. What's important to note is that we're all at different stages of our brokenness. And, when we're actively dating, the question we should ask ourselves is, "Is this someone who's doing their inner work?" I'm not certain if we're ever completely healed because there's always inner work to do, but self-awareness of one's brokenness is critical when we start to think about being in a relationship.

Most people can recognize dysfunction, but few can recognize healthy. I've encountered men who said they were ready, thought they were ready, but weren't really ready for love. I profess to be a person of quality with substance—a good man. But I haven't always been. I understand that I've been someone's disappointment at one point or another in my life.

With that, I believe in the law of reciprocity. The law of reciprocity states that what you put out always comes back to you—good or bad. It may not come from the person that you blessed, the person that you hurt, or the person that you helped, but that energy always comes back. It has to. It's like a boomerang.

So naturally, I came into contact with men who lacked emotional maturity and emotional intelligence because I was once a person who didn't possess those qualities. It's karmic energy. The disappointments that I've experienced in dating and love are from energy that I had put out, so it came back to me. I dated someone on and off for a year because he was a runner. He was more afraid of his feelings for me than he was willing to try to love me. At the height of my frustration with him, I realized that I had run in and out of a previous relationship that I was in many years before him.

Part of the reason some of my situationships didn't evolve into full-on relationships was because I refuse to participate in another relationship with a man who lacks the capacity to say how he feels, what he wants, or what he needs. Now I understand how toxic that relationship will become because I was once that guy. In previous relationships, I didn't talk about the things that bothered me because I thought it made me look weak. But it takes strength to say how you feel and to ask for what you need.

Moreover, relationships require both people involved to be teachable because in the words of Iyanla Vanzant, "Relationships are not where we go to have fun. Relationships are where we go to heal and where we go to learn." And from my perspective, if you aren't ready to heal or grow, then a relationship is not where you need to be, because relationships force us to confront those deep-seated emotional traumas. And the person that you've chosen to be in a relationship with is charged with the responsibility of helping you grow through those traumas, and vice versa. When those issues surface, you must trust your partner enough to point out the areas where you need healing. At the same time, your ego can't be more important to you than your healing because your ego will never allow your partner to teach you. It's dangerous loving someone who's more concerned with protecting their heart than opening their heart to love.

Many are intimidated by love and the raw emotions that come with being in love. I believe there's a genuine fear of love. We live in an era where most are resistant to partnerships that require monogamy. It's a culture that's littered with short term, open relationships and that seems commonplace. A big part of my reasoning for being single is that I'm interested in a long-term partnership that's monogamous, and too few of us know how to get there.

I learned the hard way that sex isn't love, and affection doesn't always equate to intimacy. Affection and intimacy are vastly different. The ability to be affectionate can exist independent of the ability to be intimate. I crave intimacy and I've dated men who were touchy feely, who enjoyed kissing and cuddling. But they couldn't handle intimate conversations about their feelings or mine because they lacked emotional intelligence and emotional maturity. I've met men that I clicked perfectly with. Yet, they still weren't ready for the responsibility of love or a relationship.

These same men were capable of reaching over to hold my hand while driving in the car or seated in a movie, but they failed at getting emotionally naked. They couldn't speak about their true feelings, which included their fears. They couldn't look me in the eyes and admit that they were in love or hurt by something I said or did. We shared similar wounds. We both were too scared to fall, too scared of looking too interested, too afraid of getting hurt again, too afraid of being cheated on, too scared to care more than the other, and the list goes on. But the only way to get to love is to walk in the direction of fear.

When your love spirit vibrates on a different frequency from what's common, it becomes a bit more challenging to find a partner, and easier to become a loner because you get comfortable with your singleness. Here's what I mean. Sometimes your gift, the calling on your life, is so great that it intimidates you as well as others, and that includes those who show up in your life with the intention of loving you—only to discover that they're too afraid of not being enough for you.

When your personality is so vivid that it swells when you enter a room, it can cause insecurities in the people around you. Or when you live a big life, it can intimidate, even scare people. That includes family, friends, the people that we date, and those with whom we find ourselves in relationships. Their fear is sometimes rooted in some insecurity that forces them to believe that you'll forget them and leave them behind. In a relationship, that kind of insecurity will convince your partner that you lack enough focus to love them because your dreams are too big. Other times it's their inability to stand with you in your light because they're threatened by your confidence. And in some cases, in an attempt to feel comfortable around you, they try to peck away at all the things that make you amazing.

What We Gain

Often, we approach relationships anticipating the reward—what we'll gain. Whether it's financial help or simply the idea of companionship itself, rather than approaching the relationship with the intention of adding value to someone else's life, we want to know what we can get. We want to know our guarantees. I have a different perspective on relationships. I'm clear that relationships aren't just about the fun stuff. It's where we go to learn more about ourselves, our partner, and life. It's the place we go to improve upon who we are. But in order to grow we must be open to learning from the partner that we've chosen to guide us in those teachable moments, without being easily frustrated, and without being so eager to leave. We have to be as willing to follow as we are to lead. That said, trust is key. We must be able to trust our partner enough to allow them to guide us to the areas of our personality that need improvement.

I remember a friend telling me, "I'd rather be alone feeling lonely than be with someone and feel like I'm by myself." I never forgot those words. She was so frustrated with her relationship because it wasn't producing the results that she craved. I was reminded that it's better to be single if being in a relationship means compromising the joy of being yourself or sacrificing peace of mind in exchange for a dead-end relationship—only to find yourself in love and lonely.

Thinking back, I believe my friend allowed her insecurities to take an active role in her love life because they influenced many of her decisions in that relationship. Sometimes we have to be okay with things not working out the way we want them to. Sometimes we have to let things be and allow people to go when they're pulling away from us, especially if things aren't falling into place.

Sometimes we stay too long because we so desperately want the relationship to work. All the signs that point to the end are there, but we can't imagine starting over with someone new. We become so tired from trying and settling in the relationship that we're left with no choice but to walk away. Part of the confusion and reason for staying beyond our breaking point is tied to the time we waste on figuring out the exact moment the relationship got off track. Truth is, there isn't always a breaking point. Sometimes it's all blurred. It all seems to run together. When there's no relief, the relationship has probably run its course.

As a kid, I was a finicky eater. More specifically, I hated when my food touched on the plate. And I refused to eat bruised fruit, you know, when apples, grapes, peaches, or bananas have those brown spots or scratches on them because they weren't handled with the most care or they were handled just a bit too rough in transport to the grocery store. This obsession still holds true today. Back then, though, whenever I complained about those bruised fruits, my mother often reminded me that everything, even fruit, has a past.

"Well, if you were packed on a truck, you'd be bruised by time you got to the grocery store too," she said that after watching me frown at the scarred fruit.

Ironically, in one section of my life I wasn't as picky with my choice in the men I dated, aside from looks. I had a tendency to gravitate to the broken ones, the ones who were in a million little pieces about their sexuality, so they spent most of their life hiding and secretly apologizing to the world for something they couldn't change. I learned firsthand that it's hard to build on broken. I write very candidly about some of those experiences in my memoir series—*Words Never Spoken: A Memoir*, and *One Thing for Certain, Two Things for Sure: A Memoir Continued.*

It's difficult making the best and brightest choices for ourselves from a place of darkness. But, it's almost impossible to write your life out on paper and remain ignorant of the poor choices you once made for yourself.

As a result of writing those books, I've since become very selective of the people with whom I share my life, platonically and romantically.

After reflecting on past dating patterns, I've become really good at choosing and eliminating because I'm comfortable with the boundaries and standards I've set for myself. I need someone who will actively participate in the health of our relationship. I want a partner who's faithful because he chooses to be, not because I police him. I no longer allow fear to convince me that better isn't possible, or that I'm asking for too much. We shouldn't have to interrogate our partner to get to the truth.

Before, fear had its way with me. It often persuaded me to believe that I had to jump at the first opportunity for a relationship that came along, because what I really wanted would never show up, because it didn't really exist. And if I didn't accept this one, then I'd end up alone.

Once upon time, I believed all relationships were inherently drama filled or dysfunctional in some way, and that I just needed to decide what type of drama I could tolerate. But that simply isn't true. Your relationship should be your place of peace, your place of refuge. It shouldn't be a place of turmoil. Some people keep up confusion in their relationship because they think consistent arguing about nothing keeps the relationship interesting. Conversely, it's exhausting, and it forces your partner to look elsewhere for calm and serenity.

I'd be willing to bet that I'm not the only person who believed that to be true—that all relationships are inherently drama filled. Otherwise, why do we stay when we know we should go? Is it fear of being alone? Are we so afraid of being alone that we'd rather suffer and tolerate the pain that comes with staying because we believe that pain is a lot easier to manage than the pain we'll feel after we leave? Perhaps. But, I would venture to say that we stay in relationships that are unhealthy, emotionally painful, loveless or empty because we don't want to feel the pain that comes after we leave. We don't want to feel the grief that comes with the loss of a relationship.

We may even go back and forth a time or two to escape the pain that comes from missing them, because the pain only seems to subside when we go back into the fold. He calls, you answer. You call or accept his call because you're hoping for different results, only to end up feeling worse because you didn't get the results you were hoping for. You take him back because it seems to erase the pain caused by the breakup. This may lessen the heartache temporarily, but oftentimes when we stay, that sadness quickly transitions into insecurities and we're unable to feel stable in the relationship because it's so fragile. So, why stay? The answer is simple. Because we're equally as afraid of joy as we are of pain. And what's the point of missing them if they're not willing to grow for you?

Everyone who comes into our life changes us, sometimes a little, sometimes a lot. Some of the people that come into our life are meant to be transitory because all love isn't intended to be a forever kind of love. Sometimes the lesson is learning how to let go. So, no matter how tight we cling to someone, they still manage to slip away despite our best efforts to hold on. Relationships are designed to grow us through the healing of each other's emotional traumas, which oftentimes stem from childhood.

I've experienced relationships that were strictly about me planting seeds for someone else to harvest and watch grow. I was simply there to pour into them. Those relationships weren't about me receiving love as much as they were about me giving love to someone who either didn't believe in love, never had love or didn't think that they deserved love. In some very special cases, it was about me giving them the tools for them heal, grow and to love someone else.

It's pointless trying to hold onto everything and everyone who shows up in your life. I'm constantly reminding myself that there are over 7 billion people living in the world. When it's intended to be lasting, it sustains without force or manipulation. If it comes and goes, it was meant to fade away. It was designed to teach you during that period of your life. Ask for the lessons to be revealed and trust them enough to let go.

Work on Gradual

There's something really sweet about gradual, but we want what we want, now and yesterday. I was in my early twenties when I began dating seriously, so there was some catching up to do, but also lots of angst. Thus, I made a few more mistakes than I wanted to.

In my mid-twenties, I briefly dated a graduate student who was working towards his Ph.D. After months of seeing each other in passing in the gym, he and I finally made direct contact and exchanged phone numbers. I remember calling him incessantly because I was an anxious twenty-something-year-old, hungry for a relationship to settle into. Thinking about it now, I'm sure part of the reason for my relentless attempts to reach him was my way of trying to lock him down before anyone else could. Sometimes we jump into situations prematurely because we fear missing out on our chance. I wanted my opportunity with him before anyone else had a chance to be with him, so I called and called and called. I left message after message hoping for a return call. But when my calls were left unanswered for weeks, I chose to believe that he wasn't interested in me, until I confronted him and learned otherwise.

I bristled when he said, "Stop making assumptions. Just because I'm not responding to you in the way that other guys have in the past, or in the way that you're used to, doesn't mean I'm not interested."

Sometimes we're so blinded by what we feel, what we think, and what we want that we forget to see someone else's perspective. He went on to say that his work and school schedules didn't leave much time for a social life, which was the reason he hadn't returned my calls. But in my head, I had already created a different story for why he hadn't called.

Nevertheless, he could have returned my call sooner, because we all make time for who and what is important to us. Still, this was a lesson for me. This wasn't as much about him as it was about me, and how paranoia convinced me that my version of the story was true, because my insecurities sponsored the story.

In fact, my insecurities sponsored more stories than I care to admit. Sometimes we create a story in our mind, and because that's the story we choose to believe, we take it as truth. Other times it's our past experiences coming back to haunt us because we haven't done that healing work on ourselves during the time that we were single.

Even after my grad student crush explained why he hadn't returned my calls, I chose to believe my version of the story. Fear had collided with insecurities and past traumas, which left me unhinged, and which provoked me to call him as many times as I had.

For a brief moment I wasn't thinking clearly or reasonably. I wasn't used to rejection. I made desperate attempts for him to see me. I wanted to be noticed. I wanted him to like me as much as I liked him. I campaigned for him to see my value—my worth. Sometimes we make desperate attempts for someone to see us when all we ever really need is to be. What I didn't realize then was that I didn't need to sell the idea of me to him—or to anyone for that matter. He was right. I had become accustomed to a certain reaction when someone was attracted to me, and his behavior didn't indicate that he liked me.

We often develop unhealthy dating patterns because of our past experiences, and what we've heard from other people about their experiences oftentimes corrupts ours. Instead of recalibrating our heart and mind to choose a better partner for ourselves, we allow our first experiences to set the tone for how we choose future partners, and how we date subsequent to that negative experience. Those unhealthy patterns force us into a type, and we begin focusing exclusively on certain traits, which limits us in an already shallow dating pool.

We set unreasonable standards and convince ourselves that he has to be a certain height, or that she has to have a particular body or hair type. He has to make a certain amount of money, and he can't have any young children. Then, we consume ourselves with choosing Mr. or Mrs. Right, only to end up choosing Mr. or Mrs. Wrong again. It's one thing to have standards, but having a "type" will keep you single or searching in a repetitive dysfunctional dating cycle that you've either adapted to or learned to crave.

We can become so accustomed to all sorts of dysfunction that it becomes impossible to recognize healthy when it finally shows up in our life. But, the beauty of patterns is that we can break them at any point once we're honest with ourselves about them. After all, happiness doesn't just happen. It's a series of good decisions. But first, we must give up on what was, so that we can finally enjoy what is.

It's difficult to appreciate what's good for us without experiencing some of the bad. I would venture to say that the ego has a more difficult time letting go than the heart does. The ego has something to prove. Ego refuses to accept that someone we want doesn't want us. Or we get upset because the person we're dating realizes, before we do, that we aren't right for each other, but the ego has trouble handling that. As a result, we refuse to let go because the ego has taken over.

I think a great deal of heartbreak is ego driven. There's a part of us, which is the ego, that has decided to conquer, tame or persuade someone to be with us after they've told us they don't want us. Or, they've demonstrated behavior to show us that they don't want us. When you're a person with lots of confidence, and you aren't used to being rejected, it can be harder to let go and walk away. Your ego convinces you that you can turn this around, to keep pushing, keep trying. You can convince him to stay. Thus, you refuse to let go, and you put forth too much effort that consequently makes you look desperate and even more undesirable. In really extreme cases, your refusal to let go can suddenly result in a fatal attraction of sorts.

We know what it looks and feels like when we're interested in someone. So, we also know what it looks and feels like when someone isn't interested in us. When pride and ego refuse to let go, we suffer because we become more determined to change someone's mind about us. There's power in letting go. Stop forcing your love onto someone who doesn't want it from you. Be strong enough to walk away, because pride will convince you to keep fighting a senseless battle.

While you're sitting there asking yourself why you're still single, consider the relationship opportunities that you may have squandered. Think of the people who were ready to love you when you weren't ready to be loved, because you weren't open to a relationship. Perhaps, you're ready today, but you weren't always.

The first time that I broke a woman's heart I was in college. It was the last relationship that I had with a woman. No, it wasn't because I realized I was gay. I felt smothered. But I also knew that I would eventually have to come to terms with my sexuality. That full story is also in my first book.

The first time that I broke a man's heart, it changed me. I never wanted to be responsible for inflicting that type of emotional pain on anyone ever again, nor did I want to experience it. I became fearful of getting into another relationship. Not just because of fear of having my heart broken, but also fear of breaking someone else's again. So, I became extremely thoughtful about how I handled another person's heart.

Breaking this man's heart wasn't intentional. It just happened. We met one night that I was out with a good friend of mine. I sent my friend over to tell him that I was interested. I cringe at the thought now of sending my friend over to speak to him for me. In fact, after we began dating, he teased me about sending someone else over to talk to him for me.

I learned a valuable lesson from that. We must go after who and what we want in life. Otherwise we're stuck with the leftovers—the ones courageous enough to approach us. And it seems like the ones with the most to lose are always the ones with the most courage to approach.

He and I began dating, but after two weeks, he asked if we could date exclusively. He showed up at my apartment one afternoon with a small gift bag. Inside the bag was a greeting card, and a toothbrush that was still in the package.

"This is for you," he said smiling.

"What is this?" I asked.

"Look inside." He had the most amazing smile, complete with the most beautiful teeth and full lips.

I pulled the card out of the bag and read it carefully. It was a simple card—nothing schmaltzy. Short and sweet. I pulled out the toothbrush. "What do you think it means?" he asked, still smiling.

"A clean start?" I asked quizzically.

"Close…I really like you Craig. I've really enjoyed getting to know you. Hopefully, we'll spend more time together, and this is my way of saying you're always welcome at my place, and hopefully I'm always welcome at your place too," he said.

I was taken aback. I was flattered. But I wasn't ready to be exclusive after only knowing him for two weeks, and I explained that to him. I didn't know enough about him. He didn't know enough about me. It's important to see a person in different shades of light to get a broader view of the person, to determine whether your relationship values and expectations align. I had never seen him upset, and he had never seen any emotion from me except happiness. It's impossible to know the fibers of your relationship without navigating some things together first—it's the only way to know if the relationship is durable.

Subsequently, I withdrew from him because I didn't know how to function any longer because he persisted despite me telling him how I felt. And, I lacked the necessary amount of emotional intelligence to be more patient with how *he* felt for me, because it was too early in our relationship. I can admit that part of it was my own fear and uncertainty about how to create a balance that was comfortable for him and me. I didn't want to be smothered again as I had been with my girlfriend in college, and I didn't want to feel like I was leading him on either.

He would leave the most melancholy voice messages—sometimes with songs playing in the background to help communicate his feelings. I felt awful that I hurt him. He was and still is a great guy, but that wasn't reason enough for me to commit so early. And just because someone is a great catch doesn't mean they're right for you.

Finding the Right Fit

One of the most difficult lessons for me was learning that just because a person is consistent and persistent doesn't mean they deserve the reward of being in a relationship with me. Everyone who wants you doesn't deserve the pleasure of having you. With that lesson, I realized that viable options for a solid partnership become fewer the more I grow. This isn't just true for me, but for anyone of substance. It seems the more education, success, and ambition one has, the more challenging it becomes to partner without feeling forced to date down.

It's become increasingly difficult to find like-minded people for relationships, but it's possible. Most come to the relationship ready to enjoy, but not ready to work. My goal is to partner with someone who will do some of the heavy emotional lifting in the relationship by meeting me in the middle, without me having to pull them there.

There's an art to dating and it begins with friendship, not sex. We've somehow gotten confused into adopting this idea that love is born out of great sex. Thus, we have sex with hopes of finding love. But, it's one thing to be ready for sex. It's another to be ready for intimacy. Intimacy requires emotional maturity, and everyone isn't equipped with that quality.

One of the challenges I've found is this genuine fear of intimacy and emotional nakedness. We don't trust each other emotionally. In the past, I gave up on love before giving it a valiant try, because the idea of trusting someone with my emotions frightened me after my first break up. Because of that first break up I always expected the story to start and end the same way. I began to anticipate deception, let downs, and other disappointments. I was too busy anticipating drama that I didn't take time to simply enjoy the moments. I wouldn't allow myself to trust that something great could actually happen to me without emotional consequences. Not because I didn't think I deserved someone great, but that I would actually be so lucky to find something that so few people in my life had found.

In one case, I dated a guy who had years of dating and relationship experience over me. I was green in comparison to him. I had never dated another man before, and he tried to use that to his advantage. Although I walked away from that experience unscathed, the residual effect on me was I expected the same behavior from everyone I dated from that point forward. The experience persuaded me to believe that it foreshadowed the behavior of every man that would come after him. Even after the dust settled and that situation was over, there was collateral emotional damage. I thought every relationship would come to a point where the game playing would begin, but that isn't so.

That relationship scarred me for years to come, and it would take years of retooling my thoughts about relationships for me to overcome those negative feelings. I had to choose to leave the baggage behind and take the lessons with me to be better for myself before I could be good for anyone else. Once I was able to separate what I knew to be true about love and relationships from what I was taught and conditioned to believe about them, the healing began. This required me to dissect what love means to me so that I could recognize it when it showed up.

The issues that I've faced with dating aren't unique by any stretch. I would never suggest that the men I dated were completely responsible for the demise of every relationship that I've had. Over the years, I've become clearer on how my behavior or response to certain situations aggravated things and contributed to various types of fallout. I've broken some hearts and my heart has been broken, so I've learned from both.

There were times that I wasn't completely open to love when the opportunity appeared in my life, or I simply wasn't as interested in them as they were in me. But I failed to communicate my disinterest, which left some of them holding onto hope. We sometimes fail to express our disinterest early on, just in case we get restless being single, or we want to revisit the possibility later down the line. But that leaves the other person holding on and wondering why they weren't enough for us.

Today, the goal of dating, for me, is love, and if it isn't leading to love, then I don't want it. What's the point of dating if your intention isn't to build towards a partnership? No relationship is going to be perfect, but there's an unspoken expectation that they're supposed to be. For most of us, the moment we see imperfection, we scurry away. So many men and women are on a forever journey to find perfection, happiness, and love only to realize at the end of their life that they could've had love all along but ran from every chance that was presented to them.

But, no one can prepare you for love. You have to show up with your guns blazing. And although heartbreak is painful, it has the potential to teach us to appreciate love when it appears again. But it takes the right kind of love for one to risk heartbreak. If you never take the risk of loving, you'll never experience its beauty.

Dating is a screening process. It's almost like a lottery, leading you to finding someone who wants what you want at the exact moment you need it. That's the secret sauce to building a great relationship. People are attracted to looks, but looks will only get you to the table. Once you're seated, the work begins. Charisma, character, confidence and personality are some of the qualities that will keep you there.

I concluded very early on that the physical type I was attracted to didn't work. I've since retired the idea that a compatible partner has to look a certain way physically. Thus, I've moved onto more important qualities. I'm more concerned with a partner who makes good decisions for himself because he's more apt to make good decisions in our relationship.

The reasons I've been single have varied. Initially, it was by choice. Later, it was a matter of trying to connect with someone with similar relationship values and expectations. Most recently, it's become my unwillingness to go along with some of the things that some men want to get away with. Integrity, consistency and emotional intelligence have ascended to the top of my list of things I need in a partner, and I actively seek those qualities when dating. Integrity is attractive because it doesn't waiver. It's a part of who we are, even when no one is watching.

I would be remiss if I didn't mention the complications of dating with the advent of social media. It's definitely changed the landscape of how we date. It's forced some to think quality is everywhere, but it isn't. Social media has tricked us into believing various illusions because everything and everyone shows up looking better online than they do in real life.

The climate and quality of your dating relationship sets the tone for the relationship itself. The person you experience while dating is the person who will show up in the relationship, because people don't really change—they only become better at hiding who they are. The person who makes their debut while you're in the getting-to-know-you phase is the same person who will have a starring role in your relationship.

Dating allows both of you a chance to decide if there's a true connection, whether or not to continue building, and the trajectory of the relationship should you decide to commit. Securing a date is the easy part. Getting to the relationship is another story. Sadly, consistency isn't rewarded—it's frowned upon. Too much interest is considered thirsty—you are either too anxious or too desperate. Yet, in my book, consistency and effort are the only ways to communicate interest. It's the only proof that we have. You can't be interested and inconsistent.

Contrary to that, inconsistency has become commonplace. For me, inconsistency is unattractive. It's as bad as being a liar. In fact, inconsistency and lying are close cousins. We've allowed our inconsistencies to communicate our disinterest in someone as opposed to just communicating that we're not interested.

Nevertheless, we hold on to some of the most unstable connections because we refuse to let the idea of being with someone go. We decide how a particular person will fit into our life and we run with the idea instead of paying attention to how they fail to show up in our life. Love isn't fickle. The one who's most interested will put forth the most effort.

Once you know your worth, you don't punish yourself by putting yourself in bad relationships. Now, we've all negotiated our standards at some point because we confused compromising with settling, and subsequently we gave more than we should have in an effort to hold onto someone. But at some point, you have to stop ignoring the signs and simply walk away. Your confidence shouldn't be tied to any man, woman or relationship.

I've always known what I bring to the table, but I lost sight of this after over-compromising a time or two. I've been guilty of saying, "I know what I deserve in a relationship," but then I didn't always require it once I actually found myself involved. After a series of revelations, I finally understood exactly what I deserved from a partner in a relationship. But I was well into my 30s when I finally discovered this. Ironically, I learned it through my friendship with my dear friend Terrence. His love is boundless. He goes out of his way to understand me and love me. He taught me through example just how effortless thoughtfulness is. It existed in the smallest gestures. I learned through our friendship how I want and need to be treated in my next relationship. And, how I should act accordingly to make my partner feel loved, too. It was interesting to see how the tables turned, and how what was once enough for me in a relationship suddenly became too little when my standards were set and in place.

Compromising in a relationship isn't a problem—settling is. Compromise should be relegated to ancillary things like what movie to see on movie night, where to have dinner, the color to paint the house—never who we are inherently. When you pretend to be someone you aren't in a relationship, you're compromising yourself, and diminishing yourself little by little.

Essentially, when you compromise yourself, you're shrinking for someone. Compromising who I am for someone is no longer an option. In a few situations, I even became too forgiving. Because of it, I was afraid to trust my instincts in love, so I chose to remain single. I couldn't seem to strike a balance between the things I should tolerate in a relationship versus those things I shouldn't.

Other times I was too unforgiving. I left no room for mistakes. There was no room for my partner to be human—to be flawed. No one is perfect. To that point, we can't expect a person to be open and honest with us if we're going to make them uncomfortable by punishing them every time they're upfront with us.

We try to train people to be in relationship with us during the course of dating, but their ideas and values for the kind of partnership they want should come close to matching yours. That way, you're not arguing about the direction the relationship moves in or its parameters. Most relationships fail because one or both people involved believe it means giving up the things they need or love for the sake of being in the relationship. As a result, they find themselves in a constant tug of war—pulling each other in opposite directions.

The boundaries that you set with your partner should be identical. Boundaries frame what's acceptable and unacceptable behavior in the relationship. They determine the terms and guidelines of your relationship for what's off limits for both of you—although your deal breakers may differ.

For example, you may not be willing to stay in your relationship if your partner cheats, but one occurrence may not be a deal breaker for your partner. Your partner may be willing to stay with you in the event you commit the infidelity. But, with boundaries, you both may agree that physical violence is the line and cause enough to end the relationship.

When your fundamental values match, it isn't necessary to force the current. Sure, there will always be tests, but we're talking about the basics. When the relationship boundaries are set, there are no debates over what's acceptable and unacceptable behavior in your relationship because you agree on those things in the beginning.

Pushing someone to adopt your position about relationships is far more difficult than finding someone who already shares your point of view. Finding quality people whose value system aligns with yours isn't easy—if it was, everyone would be in quality relationships, and no one would settle.

Standards require us to let go of what we want, sift through what's typical, and hold out for what we need until we happen upon a partner. It's popular to believe that holding onto a situationship while waiting for someone better to come along is the best solution. But this isn't true because someone is bound to get hurt and it very well may be you. Sometimes the consequence of being great, a person of substance with standards, means being single a bit longer because you refuse to settle. Other times, you just may have to admit that you're the problem because it's impossible for the problem to always be someone else, especially since you're the common denominator.

Moving Forward Through Time

When I first began having serious relationships, I had it all wrong. I thought it was innocent to spend time with someone for the sake of having something to do. I presumed attraction and commonalties were enough, as long as there was mutual interest. I thought it was ok, but sharing your time with someone is one of the most personal things we can do outside of sex. That's intimate.

Over time I learned the importance of building a relationship from friendship. It's never enough simply to have similar likes and dislikes, or attraction. It's imperative to like the person you're with outside of physicality, but when I think about it, none of my relationships in the past began that way. I would even venture to say that none of my relationships were with people I would've become friends with, but premature sex confused the kind of relationship we had. Had we not engaged in sex early on, we wouldn't have had any sort of connection—friendship or otherwise.

There's a colorful story behind every long-term relationship. And, just because a relationship looks live from the outside doesn't mean it's not dead on the inside. I ask myself a few things whenever I meet someone who's been in a relationship over the course of many years: "What compromises were made along the way?" "What sort of hurdles did they overcome?" and "What sacrifices do they make for it to work?"

Certainly, there were challenges along the way that weren't easy to navigate, but I often wonder how and why some couples are able to move past the very things that break other couples apart. My friend Danielle explained it this way, "You don't throw out brand new kitchen cabinets just because they don't fit perfectly. You sand them down, make little adjustments, and re-hang them."

Love isn't perfect, and your relationship doesn't have to be perfect either in order to bloom into something significant. Love is a dance. It's a dance that has to be learned over time. Communication is your rhythm. You have to learn your rhythm, and that starts with dating.

You don't stop dancing because your partner steps on your toe. Over time you'll learn to anticipate your partner's moves, and you'll step on each other's toes less frequently. Of course, if your partner is stepping on your toe intentionally, then of course, stop dancing. But it's another thing when it happens during the learning curve. A friend told me, "Souls do a dance, and when the music stops you feel it."

Relationships should be approached with the same fervor and ease with which we approach our friendships. Friendships aren't deliberate—they just are—without calculation. Typically, they happen organically as a result of a mutual fondness. It's the unmistaken chemistry between kindred spirits when connected, and everything snaps into place like puzzle pieces. Neither person frets or keeps score of who called whom first or last. And, no one panics over the inevitability of disagreements that may ruffle the friendship. Thus the friendship simply evolves over time without force. I had to learn that, when I'm in a relationship with someone and we disagree, I can't be focused on who's right and who's wrong, because the relationship suffers if I aim to win. My only focus should be reaching common ground.

It's impossible to get to forever without moments that challenge us or inspire us to continue working on the relationship together. With every significant relationship comes hurdles, but there's also commitment. There will be tears. We all have secret tears, but there's also some type of glue to hold us together.

Let downs will make room for benchmarks that will either make or break the bond. Moreover, the benchmarks that strengthen the relationship will help create and reinforce the foundation. Together these ingredients will galvanize the relationship, but getting to love requires a couple to adapt to whatever comes in the form of a challenge.

A mistake that many of us make with dating, and in our relationships, is telling too much of what's going on behind the scenes of the relationship to friends or family. I had a terrible habit of sharing with my friends all that was going wrong in my relationship without balancing the story with all that was great about it too.

Out of frustration, I only shared what was bothering me at that moment. I was quick to complain about what I was unhappy with, but seldom offered reports about all that was special—the things that lured me to the relationship in the first place.

Naturally, my friends' perceptions were slanted, and their attitude towards my partner was skewed, which resulted in them disliking him and offering me advice that wasn't always the best for my relationship. They offered this advice because I hadn't given them the full picture from which they could properly advise me.

We live in a world where people share more than too much on social media, which allows gossip to travel faster than good news. Everyone has his or her version of your story, but it isn't always the truth. Ultimately, some conversations should be contained within your relationship, and those things should never be discussed outside of it with anyone—good or bad—and certainly not as a Facebook status update, an Instagram post, or as a tweet on

Twitter. It's important to keep some things sacred—including intimate conversations about your sex life.

Everyone claims to be ready for a relationship until it appears. Be sure that you can handle the responsibility of love before asking for a relationship. And remember, it lasts for as long as it was meant to last. When it comes to an end, count the lessons or count it as protection, not rejection.

3 Love and Fear

*Separate your instincts and intuition from your insecurities
and fears…*

Craig Stewart

I love affection. I love love, but I'll be the first to admit
that I'm afraid of the vulnerability that comes with it. I'm
not afraid of being *in* love. I'm afraid of being there alone.
At one time in my life I used to sit around collecting the
wrongs, those possible red flags in my relationships, to
validate reasons why they wouldn't work.

I'm famous for being too methodical; thinking too far
down the line, trying to predict how the story will play
out. And, deciding whether or not to wait around to see
how things will unfold between us, or if I should run.

Discouraged by past heartbreak and intimidated by
love, I talked myself out of being in some really good
situationships that had the potential to be significant. I
even found myself starting arguments to see if my partner
cared enough to fight for us. In retrospect, it was my
attempt to avoid heartbreak by cutting the relationship off
at the path, because I was too fearful that I couldn't survive
another break up. Part of my fear was that when the
newness of the relationship wore off, the magic between us
would also dwindle, then fade. I've come to realize that it
was one of my insecurities that was steeped in fear.

For the past nine years I've been single. The first year or so I was decidedly single because it was necessary for me to recover from my last relationship. A breakup can scar us for life if we allow it. Then, no matter how great the next person is that comes into our life, we'll never see their true value to allow them room enough to love us. At least not until we've healed enough to truly see their heart and intentions. I didn't want that to be the case with me, so I took a sabbatical, of sorts, from love. I wanted to sort through what happened in my last relationship to evaluate how things went awry, so I could make better choices for myself moving forward.

There was a season in my life when I tried loving men who were severely broken. But I had to get back to a place where I could trust my own instincts when it came to love. They suffered from what's known as the broken bird syndrome. Many of them were so broken that they didn't know how to piece themselves back together again. They were bruised by past relationships, family dysfunctions, and there I was thinking I could patch them up. I was fooled or foolish enough to believe they were ready for love, prepared for an emotional connection, so I attempted to help nurse them back to a full recovery. But they weren't ready, and I was left carrying all their emotional baggage and doing all the heavy emotional lifting for them. Essentially, I was pouring love into men who were non-committal or emotionally unavailable to me.

Some of us throw love at a person's wounds. Others try to heal them by leading with gifts or money in the hope that our investment will be rewarded with a relationship. I learned the hard way that I can't heal someone's trauma or brokenness—even with my love. That's personal inner work that they must be willing to do, self-care we must all complete for ourselves.

These men weren't drawn to me because I was broken. Rather, they were attracted to my light—my spirit. They were drawn to my outlook on life and love. Some were even attracted to my dreams. It's possible for someone to be attracted to your drive, your ambition, even your career, but not to you. I used to get frustrated with myself because I have such an open heart for love despite the amount of times that I've been disappointed in relationships. But I'm grateful that I still have the capacity to love after being heartbroken, because it isn't love that I'm sick and tired of—it's the bullshit that sometimes comes with dating and relationships.

I used to question how good people who were in search of healthy relationships could find themselves in emotionally and physically volatile relationships that resulted in heartache, pain and all sorts of deception. The possibilities are endless.

We date at the level of our self-esteem. When we suffer from low self-esteem, we tend to date down. We overlook clear signs of disaster because of our need to be loved. Now, I've never suffered from low self-esteem, but I've certainly dated down, and I believe it was because I wasn't always confident with respect to dating, although I was confident in other areas of my life.

Two, monogamy is a choice if it doesn't come naturally to you. I'm a monogamous person, but I don't believe monogamy comes naturally for everyone. For some, it takes effort to be monogamous. Monogamy is a gift and it's a gift that I choose to give in my relationships. But I've definitely participated in relationships with men, that I knew going in didn't have the capacity to be monogamous. It's like we close our eyes and hope for the best. But what good is your hope when their hope is to be who they are?

Personally, I think it's unrealistic to think that in a world with over 7 billion people it doesn't require effort to be faithful—even for the most loyal people. Loyalty is one thing—commitment is another. Loyalty doesn't mean being incapable of cheating. One has to decide to be faithful. A cheater can still be loyal. A cheater isn't faithful to the relationship but can be loyal in the relationship with respect to sharing in the financial responsibilities, raising children together, sharing their life with you, and so on. This just goes to show that the two aren't mutually exclusive—cheating and loyalty can co-exist in a relationship. But is that what you want?

Monogamy is a gift that we share with a partner. But we shouldn't assume that if the bond of monogamy is broken, love is no longer there. It doesn't mean a person doesn't love you because they were unfaithful. If you've been cheated on in a relationship, you can't take it personally. It happens for a variety of reasons—some of which may have nothing to do with you. But, let's just say you've starved your partner emotionally or physically. Even in those instances, your partner made the choice to cheat as opposed to addressing the problems and leaving the relationship.

Infidelity isn't always cut and dry. People often say, "if you're not happy, why not leave the relationship?" The answer is, because it's not always about wanting to leave the relationship or to be deceptive. Sometimes cheating is a symptom of a smaller problem in the relationship and the person committing the crime, so to speak, doesn't want the relationship to be over. Rather, they're trying to escape the problem by hiding out in another relationship until there's a resolution. They may still want to be in the relationship and build a life with you.

Now, that doesn't suggest that cheating should be tolerated. The point here is that some people are wired differently. I believe monogamy is a social construct that's tied to religion and marriage. So, while most aspire to be monogamous, many will never succeed at being faithful in that way. Monogamy comes naturally to some of us, while others have to work at it.

For some, sex is just that, a physical response, and if it happens with someone outside of the relationship, it means nothing. For others, it marks the end of the relationship. Thus, if that's the kind of relationship we desire, we're charged with the responsibility of aligning with someone who also believes in monogamy.

I'm not certain if I'm made of the kind of stuff required to heal from infidelity. Not that I'm unable to, it's just that I cherish my peace of mind more. I know the kind of damage that cheating can do to one's well-being, trust, and peace of mind. I'm not one to snoop around looking for evidence of cheating, but infidelity would cause me to become that person. For example, if I called or texted my partner and didn't get a response, in what I deemed was a sufficient amount of time, I'd be concerned. I'd spazz out if he told me that he was going one place and somehow, he ended up someplace else. I could easily become someone that I don't recognize.

Third, we don't always attract similar energy. We also draw in those who want or need healing, as they're drawn to our light. We have to learn to distinguish between those who need healing, from those who are looking to complement us and want to build something significant with us. I had to learn how to separate those who were interested in me from those who were gravitating to my energy. They were fascinated by my personality, but that didn't mean they really wanted to be with me. Obviously every person who wanders into your life isn't there for you to build a life with. Some are in pain and are drawn to our light for healing, not a relationship. It was my responsibility to determine whether a particular person was brought into my life for me to love in the context of a relationship, or to love for the sake of their own healing.

We can try to love someone through their brokenness, but we must be mindful that we risk getting cut in the process, because broken glass cuts, and it can cut deeply. And, those lasting scars are the ones that we carry with us to the next relationship or dating experience. I quickly learned that my job wasn't to heal them. My responsibility was only to love them—not play therapist.

To that end, it's foolish to love someone who isn't capable or prepared to love you at the level you deserve. And that shouldn't be confused with someone loving you in the way you want to be loved because those are two different things. Just because a person doesn't love you in the way that you want them to doesn't mean that they don't love you with all they have. You must decide if the way that they love you is enough.

My life-long personal work as it relates to love involves releasing my fear of rejection. I fear opening my soul completely to someone, only for them to decide that I'm not what they want because they've changed their mind. In past relationships, I braced myself, barely breathing, taking quick breaths along the way just in case he had a change of heart.

I convinced myself, in some cases, that circumstances weren't ideal for a relationship. I decided that the timing wasn't right, things weren't perfect, it was too soon after another relationship had ended. But remember, it's possible to move from a relationship that isn't satisfying us to one that is.

Giving up on a relationship can be seen as failure, but sometimes letting go is for your own well-being, and it requires courage to let go. It's important to know the difference between giving up and letting go. Knowing when to let go of a relationship is tied to knowing when enough suddenly becomes too little. In other words, we sometimes remain in loveless relationships that aren't serving us, and we often stay because we're afraid of what singleness looks like. Or, we're simply afraid of starting over. Sometimes the answer isn't giving up. Sometimes a b-r-e-a-k is necessary for the health of a relationship. Other times, the only and best solution is simply to let go—never to look back.

There's an unspoken relationship between love and fear. Most will say they want love, they're ready for love, until it shows up. We crave love, then shy away from it once we get there. We're so beautifully complicated. We chase love, but at our core we're afraid of it once we catch up to it, once love shows itself. It seems that love never comes packaged the way that we expect, and not just physically.

Love will stretch us beyond our expectations. It's designed to do that. Love humbles us, and I believe our fear of love is misdirected. We really fear heartache as a result of love breaking down. Many relationships fail because we anticipate being disappointed or betrayed by our partner. We anticipate things that will destroy the union. Other times, we put things in motion ourselves that cause us to break up, like a self-fulfilling prophecy.

Love and fear seem inextricably bound, almost coalescing, when it comes to relationship groundwork. But there has to be a tradeoff to prevent the pair from working together. Fear has to yield to allow love in. Otherwise, we will convince ourselves to give up before we even get started.

Fear has the ability to eclipse love. Fear cripples. Fear damages. Fear stunts growth. Fear keeps us from being free. Fear prevents us from living our truth. Fear sways us to believe things are worse than they are. Fear can cost you love. Fear blocks love. But, the only way to get to love is to risk a broken heart. It takes more effort and energy to hold onto your heart than to make it available to love. Of course, that doesn't mean you should give it all away. Save some for yourself too.

Few people experience the purest form of love. They lack the courage required to push past that wall of fear that they've built as protection, but that same wall could ultimately destroy their chances to love. We approach that wall, then turn away. We're afraid to move beyond the uncertainty because the unknown scares us.

The emotional scars from my first long-term relationship crippled every thought I had of trying love again. I figured I wasn't meant to be in a long-term relationship, although I knew I was capable of the commitment and sacrifice required for one. It was fear talking.

To one degree or another, a trauma occurs with every breakup, and they alter and shape who we become. I've watched men that I loved go on to live out the dreams that I had for us with someone else. Still, I got to decide if I would be better or worse because of them. I chose to be better.

I developed a pattern of unconsciously dating men who were severely closeted. In hindsight, I realize that this was a pattern associated with a defense mechanism I had developed for me to avoid heartbreak again. There was a part of me that knew these men weren't looking for anything long-term, so in that regard the interaction felt safe because there would never be a breakup to grieve, so to speak. A relationship wasn't the end goal for either of us. I gravitated to men who weren't interested in building a relationship because I thought it offered me some protection. I knew there would never be conversations about moving forward with a more serious connection, so it felt safe.

Defense mechanisms, no matter how they are demonstrated in our life, are products of fear. My fear has almost paralyzed any thought that I've had of allowing myself the freedom to love openly and fully to experience love's bounty. At the same time, I've always held onto my hope tighter than my doubts. I've always secretly believed in the possibility of love.

Each of us has defense mechanisms to protect us from emotional trauma. My instinctive reflex to guard my emotions could be compared to the way in which muscles spasm in our back to protect the spine from trauma when involved in a car accident.

Some self-protect by counting the reasons it will never work instead of relaxing into the relationship. Some hold back affection—refusing to say, "I love you," until their partner says it first. It's a game that we play with ourselves and our partner, whether they realize it or not. We all demonstrate fear differently. Some of us shy away from vulnerability because we're no longer in control of our emotions, while others secretly sabotage love by straying from the relationship or convincing themselves that something is missing.

I once dated a guy who pulled away from me periodically when his feelings for me began to overtake him. He told me that he hadn't expected to like me as quickly as he had. Pulling away became his way of trying to manage his emotions and regain self-control. He said that he was terrified to love me and that I reminded him that he still had trust issues to work through from a previous relationship. He also said that he felt safe with me. Nevertheless, he wouldn't allow himself the freedom to love me with his whole heart because he was paralyzed by fear. He was broken from relationships that didn't work out, and some family dynamics that had left him scarred.

I tried to show him that it was safe to love me, but I realized that he wasn't ready. I never doubted his feelings for me because they were clear, but his trepidation was equally apparent. I had to get honest with myself. Part of the reason that I held on, through the pain of it all, was fear of losing him to someone else. I was afraid to let him go because I was scared that he would become ready to love again, and I wouldn't be around to share it with him. I didn't want him to forget about me or what we had, so I held on even after I knew I needed to let him go. I realized that letting him go was my only real option at the time.

He'd never had someone to love him without expectation or reciprocity. His defenses instructed him to push me away. Consistency scared him because he feared acclimating to it, only to lose it later down the line should things between us fall apart. He didn't want to become accustomed to something or someone who may only be there temporarily. He was so afraid of losing me that he chose to pull away before he could get comfortable having me. He'd never been able to count on love. Thus, he even insisted that we remain friends so that if the relationship didn't work, he could at least have me as a friend forever.

His wall, his defense mechanism, was to run because he didn't believe that he was worthy or deserving of something he had never experienced. And some of what was showing up between us in the relationship was his childhood trauma. I once heard someone say, "Being an adult is about healing childhood trauma."

We all come to our relationship experiences carrying our childhood trauma because it inevitably shows up in some form or another.

There were times that I was ready to give up on this man sooner than I had, but I shared my struggles with a friend, and she pushed me to keep trying. There's something to be said about a woman's approach to love in a relationship. It's relentless. She encouraged me to try a different approach when I wanted to throw in the towel and walk away. She even asked for me to pray for him because he and I would both be better off because of it, even if we didn't end up together. Her advice was sound, and it was doable. It didn't cost me anything but effort. It wasn't humiliating or degrading. It was honest and sincere. He was worth it.

Instead of turning away from him I chose to love him through his fear. No, I didn't put my life on hold. I decided to step back, to give him space and enough room, to choose me for himself, rather than torturing myself by making more attempts to spend time with him. I never tried to convince him that we could be perfect together. That was up to him to see. There were other lessons in this process for me.

He challenged me to be more myself, to grow to another level to really earn love, which is a lesson that comes with dating. Patience has always been my Achilles heel in life, especially in love. This man taught me another level of patience. I became more disciplined and learned to harness my ego by not allowing myself to take things personally. Because I loved him, I respected him enough to give him what he really needed and what he asked for at that time—friendship.

See, the problem many of us have with love is that we expect the person that we're dating to reach the finish line at the same moment we arrive. And if they don't, we get frantic, then frustrated, and oftentimes we pull away. We become bitter because we didn't get what we wanted.

Although he'd pursued me when we first met, he also told me that he was interested in building a friendship first to see if we could build upon that. Yes, I reached the finish line first. I knew that I was ready for more than friendship before he did; at least that's the way it seemed. After five months of dating, building with, and learning about each other, I was ready to commit. I was ready for the relationship. He wasn't. Or if he was, he never admitted it.

I got frustrated with the process, but never allowed myself to force him along, nor did I walk away from him because I was angry. I acknowledged where he was in the process and I chose to love him anyway because I felt he was worth it, but my life went on.

Fear dictated every calculated move that he made towards me, and away from me. He tried convincing himself and me that I'd be better off without him. His insecurities wouldn't allow him to believe that he was enough for me, but love pulled and tugged at his heart.

Again, love isn't just about the fun stuff. My friend that was counseling me reminded me to, "Love him. Learn him. Love him more. Don't abandon him when it's hard." And so I tried. Relationships are about building and growing together. I showed him who I am, and in time he showed me who he was. We became better for each other. That's growth. That's partnership. That's love.

Our fears sometimes speak louder than our hope. Fear can only paralyze us if we allow ourselves to hear doubt louder than hope. Fear stems from emotional pain. My fears about love emerged after my parents divorced. I thought their experiences would subsequently become my own.

Recently, I uncovered the reasons why I was afraid to label past relationships as such—despite the fact that we were already functioning that way. In one case, I was living with a guy. Yet, whenever someone asked, I still didn't consider it a relationship. I feared that we would become complacent; that he would get so comfortable with me that his feelings would wane. I was afraid of our lives becoming mundane and that he would take me for granted. I still worry that I will not know which relationship issues to confront and which I shouldn't, when to push and when to pull, when to yield and when to proceed. I'm nervous that I may forget to leave room for us both to make mistakes—to be human. After all, yesterday's mistakes are today's lessons, and tomorrow's answers.

For most of us, the ego dictates how we love or the quality of love that we give. We're also influenced by the culture around us. We sometimes adopt the experiences of our family and friends, and that fear resides in us long before, and sometimes after, we enter into a relationship. And when relationships around us crumble, we fear that the pendulum is swinging towards our relationship next.

Our personal experiences with emotional pain play a part in what we believe about love, as do the relationships that are modeled by our family. Even the music that we listen to shapes our perception of love positively or negatively. My music playlist once consisted of many sad and lonely songs that were well-written, but they affected my spirit, my energy, and my outlook on love. Subsequently, I created a playlist with more balance. I quickly added songs that would speak to my soul in an uplifting and vibrant way.

Fear of loving deeply and intimately is rooted in a variety of insecurities. We don't have to be insecure people for insecurities to shine through. We all have insecurities to some degree—it's human. Insecurities cajole us into believing something to be true that isn't. For example, insecurities fuel trust issues and persuade us to believe our partner is cheating because insecurity intensifies jealousy and suspicion.

Another insecurity is fear of not getting back the love that we give, followed by a fear that someone better will come along and snatch love from us once we've found it. We're constantly comparing ourselves to others for one reason or another. Insecurities kill relationships, because no matter how much or how often our partner tries to affirm us, it'll never be enough.

Oftentimes we settle into relationships that are safe, relationships that don't challenge us because they're easy. We spend years grazing in various relationships that don't fulfill us—staying in the relationship until something better comes along. Staying because we're unsure of who we are outside of a relationship with someone. We have to make a choice, to be in love or to be afraid, but it's impossible to do both. Just as it's impossible to fall in love with someone you pity.

When your mind wanders to that negative place, simply shift those thoughts to something positive. Nothing good comes from insecurities in a relationship. If you both carry extreme insecurities with you into the relationship, it will only create cycles of continuous hurt for each other. You'll spend the duration of the relationship trying to prove your love to one another.

Sometimes it seems these days that dysfunction is more attractive than normalcy. I've witnessed people disrupt perfectly healthy relationships because there wasn't enough drama for them to feel like it was real. Dysfunction was missing. And some are so used to dysfunction that without it they don't know how to exist in the relationship because dysfunction has become their normal.

It's imperative to do the self-healing work before trying to be with someone to avoid placing blame on them for things that you have left unresolved. In several of my past relationships I played counselor instead of being a partner. It's almost impossible to repair your insecurities while in a relationship because the burden typically falls on your partner to reassure you of their love, that he or she wants what you want, and that they're faithful.

We regard our relationships as possessions. We set expectations for our partner—how they should act, how they should live, even who they're friends with—as if they no longer have a say because now they're in a relationship with us. And if, for some reason, our partner does the opposite of what we want, or what we deem to be appropriate, then we assume that it somehow reflects on how they prioritize the importance of the relationship.

Love is not control or ownership. Love is freedom, with clear boundaries that define the lines of respect in the relationship. When we try to control our partner, that's our insecurities controlling us. Sometimes in an effort to protect our relationship and our emotions, we smother love. We cling too tightly. When we crowd love, it suffocates. Whenever I feel myself squeezing love or the life out of a relationship by holding on too tightly, I ask myself a few things, "What are you afraid of?" "Which of your insecurities does this speak to?' and "What does this say about you?"

Despite the amount of work that we do on ourselves, a love relationship with an ideal partner will always offer opportunities to see things about ourselves that we could never see on our own. Some relationships are for the sole purpose of allowing us to see ourselves for who we really are through the lens of that relationship. I had experiences that were only intended to provide me with lessons to extrapolate wisdom for future use, but I've also had those that were reflections of me. The qualities that I needed to see about myself, I saw through my partner.

Love is more than a feeling or the ability to say it—it's the ability to demonstrate it without fear. It's in our actions, as often as possible in a touch, a look, or a smile. When we touch a person's heart it's limitless—that's love.

Love is possible for all of us because life would be unfair if we all weren't given the chance to experience love deliriously. The questions to ask yourself are, "Will I recognize love when it shows up in my life?" and "Will I be ready?" because we're all functionally dysfunctional at times.

Some of us have learned how to be and who to be as individuals but we're clueless about who and how to be with someone else. We say we want love, true love, until it shows up at our front door and it then challenges us on every level.

At times we shudder at love, we second-guess it, we pick at it until we pull it apart. We question it, even sabotage it by doing something to threaten our chance to be with someone, including cheating.

We doubt love, even when it's better than anything we've ever experienced or witnessed before. When it feels too perfect, we manage to act up and act out because of fear, or because it doesn't look, feel, or show up the way we imagined it in our dreams. We say that we want to be with someone, but then run because we're afraid of not being enough. Sometimes it feels easier to go in and out of situations as opposed to committing.

But, a life without love isn't a life at all. The beauty of life is that we can change our mind about anything at any given time, including the experience of fear and our negative ideas about love, because we control what we think.

The vulnerability required for love—to stay, settle down, open up and confront our deepest emotions—is what's needed to heal our insecurities that center on love. Part of our happiness is tied to being with someone in a relationship, although we live in a world that says it's codependent.

I'm very specific, yet undecided about many things. But I'm clear on how I need to be loved. I need to be loved through my past, and the issues that I still carry with me because of my past. Love me enough to see past my past. I need to be loved through the layers as I continue to heal my fears about love.

Love is gentle. It's careful with our feelings, and it doesn't seek to get even. Love gives us courage to confront, then acknowledge, our weaknesses so we can improve. Love stretches us to our limit and to our fullest potential. If your love experience doesn't do that for you, then it isn't love.

Remember what you bring to the relationship. It's imperative to maintain a level of respect. Challenge yourself to show up, knowing that you are enough. Relax and let it be. Don't force a connection because you're tired of being single. It'll happen when it's meant to be.

I've begun praying a simple prayer, "Make me the person You want me to be, for the person that You have for me to love."

Which will you choose? Love or fear?

4 Difficult Conversations

Conversation and confrontation aren't the same...

Craig Stewart

Every relationship has benchmarks, and they are designed to either build or break the bond that connects us to a family member, a friend, or someone in a romantic relationship. It's these crossroads that we face in every relationship that will lead us to honest conversations that can be tough to have, but necessary just the same. I believe we can get away with saying anything to anyone. It's just a matter of how we say it.

I was involved in a car crash that resulted in a falling out with a friend. I was a passenger in his car. We were headed to the gym one morning when it happened. I had a habit of looking over his shoulder whenever I rode with him because, in my opinion, he wasn't a very present driver, which I often told him. He was easily distracted and a bit paranoid behind the wheel. Part of it could've been because he had recently relocated to Georgia from California, where we met.

When he first moved to Georgia, he was living about an hour outside of Atlanta, but most of his life existed in the city, which meant he commuted into the city every day. I offered him a place to stay for a few months because my place was centrally located, but by the time of the accident he had moved into a place of his own.

As we were driving to the gym, he began searching through his phone for something on YouTube, so his attention was divided. He attempted to change lanes, but he didn't look before doing so. Out of my peripheral vision, I noticed a dark-colored vehicle in the left lane just as he was merging into that lane. Before I could warn him, we collided. We ricocheted off the SUV, then crossed back over into the lane that we were in originally. Then we careened off the road.

There was a tree in my direct line of sight. I saw my life flash before my eyes. All I could imagine was the tree coming through the windshield and impaling me, or the windshield shattering and cutting me to death. I covered my face and hoped for the best.

When I was about seven, my parents were involved in a near fatal car crash. At the time, my mother didn't drive. My father was taking her to work when another driver ran a red light. I was visiting at a neighbor's house when it happened. My friend's mother received a call that I needed to return home, and when I did my parents were both bandaged and bruised. My father looked like a mummy. His head and eyes were covered with gauze because there were shards of glass in his eyes. I was hysterical. I thought he would be blind permanently. But the doctors had told him that the glass pieces would eventually remove themselves after several weeks.

During my own accident, as the dust from the airbag settled, I could see that my hand was cut in six places and I was bleeding profusely. I was scrambling to find my cell phone to dial 911. Blood dripped from my hand and it was beginning to feel numb from the cold January air.

When the airbag deployed it had smacked me in the face. Dust from the airbag filled the car and I could barely see. I'm guessing the airbag was responsible for the cuts on my hand because my face was burning from what felt like a carpet burn. Most of the impact occurred on my side of the car, so the passenger side door was jammed when I tried to get out.

My cell phone fell between the seat and the console. I reached for it and called 911. I could see an older White man running up to my side of the car. He pulled on the door and it dislodged. "Is everyone ok in there?" he asked.

"Yes," I said in a muffled voice.

The 911 operator was collecting information from me to send help.

"I've already called for help," the man said.

"Sir, don't hang up! He didn't give us the make and model of the cars," the operator explained.

When I finally stepped out of the car, the EMTs had arrived. The tree had crushed my friend's red sports coupe like an aluminum can. It was apparent that his car was totaled, as was the woman's Lexus truck that we hit. The tree, on the other hand, was still standing tall with what appeared to be just a few nicks and gashes from the collision.

"Is everyone ok? Do you need an ambulance?" one of the technicians asked.

"No, I'm ok," I mumbled.

Deep down I wanted to say that I needed to go to the hospital because I knew I wasn't ok. They began bandaging my hand immediately. I had a knot on my shin, and I was limping slightly. Still, I refused medical treatment.

Two of the emergency technicians tried to encourage me to go to the hospital by reminding me that we had hit a tree. They insisted that I would feel the pain once the adrenaline stopped pumping through my body. One of the technicians went on to say that we were lucky to be alive. He added that he had never seen someone walk away from an accident as severe as this one.

My hesitation wasn't for fear of hospitals or doctors, but concern about my friend's insurance rate increasing because he was responsible for the accident. And I knew that he didn't have money to pay out of pocket for the medical bills that were going to be created. But in the time it took for the EMT to arrive, and the police to come and take a report, an hour had passed, and I was in pain. I was left with no choice but to seek medical treatment. I could barely stand up straight. Luckily, a passerby, who witnessed the accident, offered to take me to the hospital since I had turned down the ambulance. The drive to the hospital was as bumpy as it was painful.

My visit to the emergency room proved to be worthwhile. Aside from the knot on my shin and the lacerations to my right hand, the x-rays and MRI showed a sprained ankle. I also had swollen muscles and tissues in my shoulders, neck, and elbow down to my left hand, which prevented me from closing my fingers to a fist. I was prescribed pain relievers and muscle relaxers before I was sent home.

Later that day, my friend called to apologize again for the accident. He was so apologetic at the scene of the accident that he was almost brought to tears. I told him not to worry, and added that I was just grateful it wasn't worse than it was. There were no broken bones, and no one was paralyzed or killed. We had a lot to be grateful for that day.

On the call, he also mentioned that his insurance company would be calling me for a statement, and that they were accepting full responsibility for the accident. When his insurance company called for my statement, they made a $1,500 offer and they agreed to pay up to $5,000 in medical expenses, but it didn't make sense for me to accept their offer because I hadn't begun my chiropractic treatments, so I declined. I had no way of predicting what the medical bills would be once all was said and done.

Ultimately, I hired an attorney to sue his insurance company because I was hurt and there were medical expenses that far exceeded their offer. Suing my friend's insurance company was the only option to cover those bills, which is the reason we carry insurance. I reached out to my friend in the days, weeks and months that followed the car accident, but our interaction was intermittent. I suggested on multiple occasions that we meet to talk, but he never committed to a sit down on the occasions that he responded. Eventually, I gave up. It's a conversation still waiting to happen. I never heard from him again.

The stakes are higher when difficult conversations are tethered to social and political issues because there's a standard of accountability. As a culture, we've become so politically sensitive and correct, that we're afraid to say the things we want to say, and afraid to ask the things we want to know out of fear of offending individuals, communities, or groups of people. Most people would rather say nothing than to risk sounding ignorant, insensitive, racist, misogynistic, or homophobic. It's the reason White folks avoid conversations about racism with Black people. It's the reason heterosexual people shy away from putting forth any true effort in trying to understand gayness. Instead, they'd rather visit the burden of changing, through prayer of course, on gay people. And let's not forget gay people who avoid and malign trans people although trans people exist within the same subculture and are marginalized in similar ways that gay people are.

There's been a lot of conversation in recent years about White privilege and bringing those benefits of whiteness to the attention of White folks for the purpose of allowing them to see racism and their advantages over Black people through the lenses of Black people in this country. This work is critical, crucial, and very much necessary, but the truth is, there are privileges in every community and it's important that each of us is aware of the privileges that we possess.

For example, we can all agree that the trans community is highly misunderstood and often persecuted. Nevertheless, there are trans men and women who have transitioned so that their outer appearance matches the feelings that they have on the inside. Thus, they're able to enjoy privileges that other trans people cannot because they are now able to pass without anyone knowing they are trans. To that point, they're able to function in the world and navigate day to day without incidents of violence or discrimination. But there are many trans people who are unable to pass and are sometimes killed or forced into sex work because they're not afforded the same employment opportunities.

If we're thinking critically and being intellectually honest, we can admit that we're all guilty of avoiding the tough conversations until we're forced to address them. A classic example of this happens often between celebrities and non-celebrities. We saw this demonstrated after Kevin Hart was condemned for a homophobic tweet that he sent almost a decade ago. Was the tweet offensive? Yes, it was. And it's the sort of vitriol that has the potential to influence a parent to disown their child or push someone to commit suicide.

Because of his celebrity, we hold him to a higher moral standard. His tweet was sent years before this public outrage occurred, which meant that at the time that it was sent, his comments weren't viewed by the general public as offensive enough to create such a commotion. So, what does that say about who we were as a society at that time that we could allow his remarks to slide? Obviously, our society was a different place then, and we weren't as inclusive of LGBTQ people, because there was no kerfuffle. So, instead of addressing that truth, we focused on punishing and persecuting Hart for something that many people believed about gay people at that time in our society.

Personally, I think it's unfair to try to ruin someone's life or career because they don't share our views. Just don't support them if you feel strongly about a particular issue. But in this case, he apologized. Now, whether or not his apology was sincere or mere damage control to protect his career, I don't know. But what I do know is that we have to leave room for people to be flawed, to be human, to grow and to evolve. We've all made mistakes that we need to recover from, but we fail to give each other the latitude to grow, because it's easier to assume that we are incapable of changing. So, we punish each other for having different biases and politics.

At the base of racism, classism, sexism, and homophobia are difficult conversations that need to happen, and the key to understanding people who are different from us is through conversation. From a spiritual perspective, I believe one of the biggest responsibilities we have while here on earth, living with so many differences, is to sort through them and grow together.

I read a Facebook post that said, "Speak the truth even if your voice shakes." It reminded me of conversations I was too afraid to have in my personal life, conversations that I should've had but didn't. It challenged me to face my fears by broaching those conversations head on.

When Kanye West professed that slavery was a choice, Black people across this country were outraged and embarrassed, to say the least. I wasn't. I did not agree, but I understood what he was trying to articulate. What I understood him saying was that slavery existed for as long as it did because we were not in sync as a people—much like today in many ways.

Sure, there were other variables involved that ensured our enslavement, like the fact that the colonizers had access to weapons, and we were unfamiliar with the land and the language. But ultimately, I believe it was our frustration with the system of slavery that helped us unlock those shackles to slavery. Once enough of us made the decision to take our freedom back, the battle began. The situation was similar to what has to happen and will happen with Black people in this country today as it relates to systems of racism. Now that isn't to simplify or reduce the effects of slavery or racism by any means, but merely to suggest that Kanye chose his words poorly.

When the news broke that rapper Nipsey Hussle was killed by another Black man, the same type of senseless violence that's shaking communities of color across this country, many were shocked. They wanted to believe that there was a government conspiracy theory to take out male members of the Black community. Not that conspiracy theories are too far-fetched, because America has certainly participated in her share, but it was interesting to see so many Black people taking to social media with their minds made up that the only logical answer was that a government agency was behind Hussle's death. But the truth was, another Black man wanted him dead.

It's always easier to point the finger away from self, easier to blame someone or something for everything. There's work that we have to do as Black people, and I understand the layers—the systemic, generational, and socioeconomic factors. But even after all that's said and done, we have some things to heal within the Black family – between Black men and Black women, with Black gay people and Black heterosexual people, Black gay men and Black heterosexual men, Black gay men and Black women, and within the Black LGBTQ community – because the truth is we don't always like each other within our community. And, most of the healing that we must do as Black people collectively begins and ends with the Black church.

A first step to bridging these divides is to realize that we are Black first and each of our lives matter, irrespective of our individual experiences, sexuality, gender, socioeconomic background, and education (because we sometimes look down on those in the Black community that are uneducated). When one of us dies, we all die, and that's whether you're gay, straight or trans. Black Lives won't truly matter until we all matter to each other, and that includes loving and supporting Black LGBTQ people.

Another truth that I've had to get honest with myself about is that there are Black gay men who have abandoned the Black gay community because we hurt them—the Black church, the Black family, the Black community, and even the Black gay community. We have to own that truth. But it's easier for some of us to believe that these men opted to date and find love outside of the Black gay community because they've sold out.

The reality is, not all Black gay men left the Black gay community because of self-hate or identity issues with their Black skin. Some felt forced out by us. Some separated themselves from us because it was too painful to stay. We teased them, humiliated them for being too soft, punched, kicked and spit on them because of who they were. We hated them. We called them sissy, punk and fag, long before a White person ever had a chance to call them nigger. Leaving was best, for their own peace of mind and well-being. Nothing is ever completely black or white.

I had a conversation with a friend about the things that I deem to be our obligation to the Black community, but we had different opinions. We agreed that the community that should've embraced us first, and our work as artists, should've been Black people because we are Black. But we were both very clear that Black folks were not always first in line to support the art that we create or the businesses that we built.

In both of our experiences we received that initial support from people that didn't look like us—they were White people. I shared with my friend that I had practically campaigned to get exposure for my work in *Essence* magazine—a Black woman's beauty bible—to no avail. Even with help from friends who work within the company, it was impossible to get the powers that be to see me or my work for that matter.

With respect to my stage play, memoirs, and my greeting card company, I received the same emphatic "no" each time. I was told over and over again that my stage play and books were too gay, and *Essence* magazine wasn't interested in talking about the gay issue.

I understood my friend's point of view and her pain because I've felt overlooked at one point only to feel welcomed later. It feels disingenuous when the Black media and the Black community claim you as their own after refusing you, previously. Suddenly, they want to celebrate your achievements and highlight your accomplishments after only a few wins in the mainstream.

Nevertheless, I was clear that I couldn't punish the entire Black community by refusing to reach back to help or support others because a handful of Black people refused to help me. My loyalty didn't hinge on how I was treated. I refused to turn my back on the entire community because a crop of Black people that could've helped me in the beginning didn't.

My friend's perspective was different. She felt no obligation to the Black community because her pain ran deep, from the anvil she believed Black folks dropped on her back at every stage of her career as she tried to climb forward. The only relief she recalls came from White people who gave her a chance to move forward. I reminded her that although she may not have felt supported by Black people as a whole initially, her core support has always come from Black women. There were Black gatekeepers who may have blocked her from certain opportunities, but her support was from Black women.

It's important to note that people from every community experience these same feelings of a lack of support from within their respective community. This isn't specific to Black people or the Black community. There is, however, a myth that's been embedded within the Black community that we must have the support of the White dollar in order for a Black owned business to prosper. And oftentimes Black business owners go out of their way to secure support from outside the Black community because they believe it's the only way they'll be able to keep their doors open, and their business will flourish. I've experienced first-hand subpar customer service from Black owned businesses, while witnessing five-star customer service being delivered to the White customer standing in front of me.

The reality is, Black people are enough to sustain Black owned businesses when we make a concerted effort to support each other. There are multimillion-dollar businesses and multibillion-dollar industries that sustain primarily off the Black dollar. It's time that we do better and be better for each other.

5 Envy

Gratitude leaves no room envy…

Craig Stewart

In the book, *A Course in Miracles,* the author, Helen Schucman, says, "When you give to others to the degree that you sacrifice yourself, you make the other person a thief…because they're stealing from you what you need, and they don't even know it."

To that end, several years ago, I heard spiritual teacher and life coach Iyanla Vanzant say to Oprah Winfrey in a conversation, "What comes out of the cup is for y'all. What's in the cup is mine." We must be as good as possible to ourselves, first, in order to be of service to others. That's growth.

As children, we're taught to always be nice, play nicely, and share. And, as we form as adults, we believe that we must always share our time and possessions with everyone around us when asked. It's almost like we're predisposed to people pleasing. I no longer believe that.

I do believe that people often confuse bragging with celebrating oneself. There's a vast difference between bragging and celebrating oneself. Bragging is connected to insecurities, and it's defined as excessive talk about oneself, one's achievements or possessions. That's different from having pride in yourself because you achieved something or overcame difficulties.

I can remember as a child being excited about getting a new pair of sneakers or scoring perfectly on an assignment at school, but feeling like I couldn't celebrate openly. My parents were always ecstatic and happy to hear about my good news, but my father discouraged me from sharing too much with my friends or cousins. He thought that they might get the wrong impression and feel like I was being boastful.

I was taught not to speak too openly or boldly about the things that I had or the things that I accomplished because it would be perceived as bragging. And, my dad in particular, didn't want my cousins to feel less fortunate if I had something that their parents weren't in a position to give them.

In hindsight, I understand his reasoning, but it confused me for a bit because I started to believe that I couldn't openly acknowledge the things I did well. I carried that belief throughout most of my young adult life, which resulted in me shrinking, in many spaces, out of fear I would be perceived as trying to overshadow other people.

During that time, I minimized my accomplishments because I didn't want to be misunderstood or mislabeled as self-centered, or any of the other things that people say when they're intimidated by you. What I know is that people are either inspired by you or intimidated because of you. The truth is, people who feel equally as accomplished as you are don't grade you in that way. There is no in between. When someone is confident in who they are and what they have, they're not threatened by you or all that you have to offer. I know for sure that confident people aren't intimidated by confident people.

Sometimes it's easy to feel like we can never celebrate our accomplishments with the people that are most important to us, whether it's for a promotion at a job, a raise in salary, a new relationship, the purchase of a new home or any other success. Essentially, many of us were indirectly taught to dim our own light.

Think about the times in your life that you knew you were better suited for something or more knowledgeable about a particular task, but you took a back seat instead of speaking up and taking the lead because you didn't want to be perceived as pushy or bossy. Now, think about the times that someone paid you a compliment and you shied away from it by pointing out a flaw, or you became embarrassed.

Our White counterparts have been taught the opposite. As children, they're praised for everything from the smallest to the most significant things they do, which may explain some of the entitlements and privileges that many White folks enjoy. This isn't to suggest that Black folks should model or emulate White people. Rather, it's more of an observation.

These revelations about growth were revealed to me during what I call my incubation and isolation period. There's a point in life when we're all forced to face an involuntary isolation in order to come out on the other side renewed. For me, this was a time of replacing and repairing. It was a space in time that allowed me to slow down and pay closer attention to my life and who I had participating in my life. I had reached a breaking point. I released people and things that once carried value to me.

This period of extreme solitude allowed me to re-evaluate my life. It was lonely because I was transitioning from one phase of life to the next, and I was forced to leave behind people who were once a support system for me. Unfortunately, some of those relationships had become stale, even toxic, but I didn't see it as losing friends. I was removing snakes. I was growing in a new direction and the only way I would get to see and experience a new level of growth was to detach myself from them and commit to a spiritual quarantine indefinitely. The end result for me was the birth of my first book, and the realization that it all happened by design.

I've been challenging myself to acknowledge, celebrate, and embrace my accomplishments without fear of being graded negatively by others. Not in an obnoxious way, but in a serendipitous kind of way. If it works its way into the conversation, then I don't shy away from expressing my wins, my victories, or my attributes by dimming my own light. There was a time that compliments made me uncomfortable, but I've learned to accept them gracefully, without pointing out a flaw to neutralize the compliment.

6 Passion, Fate, and Destiny

Sometimes we have to be seemingly off course in order to find our path in life...

Craig Stewart

Most of us believe we can force movement in our career to create success. In actuality, there's a fine line between what we can manipulate and what is based on fate. I believe everything happens when and as it should, but there's a very specific dose of knowing when to control the reins of your life, and when to allow life itself to lead or happen on its own. The most difficult part for us, I believe, is deciding when to do one over the other.

Success requires the right amount of nudging and manipulation from us, and the perfect dose of serendipity, chance, and timing. Too much force can be detrimental to our peace of mind. When we obsess over a thing, oftentimes, we begin to push too much, which costs us results. And when we fail to see the results that we anticipate, we become frustrated and begin to feel defeated.

I remember being in very desperate financial circumstances which resulted in me panicking. When I panicked, I made poor choices and decisions—and that was true in every area of my life. When we panic, we fail to see the obvious, and we lose sight of our sense of creativeness and resourcefulness to finagle our way through or around things because our mind is burdened by fear of things not happening the way we desire.

And, when we fail to push enough it's easy to slip into complacency. We become lackadaisical and unproductive because some believe fate is magic. Some of us rest on this idea that things will happen automatically, with little to no effort from us because we tell ourselves "whatever's meant to be, will be." But, the unspoken part of that affirmation is, "…if you do your part."

Do your part, all that you can do to invest in your passion, but remember to live also. I used to punish myself because my dream seemed to be at a standstill, and I thought any time away from "doing the work" meant that I was slacking. Thus, I worked tirelessly trying to speed things up, which left me with very little time for extracurricular activities with friends and family.

It's okay to pour yourself into your dream completely but allow the dream to breathe also. Step away from it so that you can see the dream with fresh eyes. When we take time to recalibrate, we can return to the journey with a clearer path and an open mind.

When a person bounces from job to job, monkey barring from one career to the next, or they scramble from one big idea to another, it's usually because they have no idea what they were called to do as their life work. They have an abundance of ideas that seem to pop up out of nowhere and they're genuinely excited about each idea. But they have no clue what their purpose or passion is. In truth, their soul is searching for its purpose.

I've known my purpose for some time now. Yet, there were times in my life that I couldn't seem to maintain a fulltime job to sustain and finance my dream. I believe this was God's way of keeping me on course to my destiny, so my focus wouldn't become just any old job. Instead, I would always keep my eyes on my life's purpose. The longest I've held any position was 14 months.

In 2002, I wrote and produced a stage play called *A Day in the Life*. The subject matter centered on issues that affect gay men. The debut show sold out, but the second and third productions flopped, and the last production in 2007 opened to a sold-out audience. Still, I could never seem to garner enough support to tour the show nationally, which was my ultimate goal. I couldn't seem to gain enough interest from promoters, corporate sponsors, or investors to fund a national tour because of the subject matter. The potential sponsors believed the world wasn't ready for such a storyline. It was pretty taboo in the early 2000s for a show of any kind to feature LGBTQ characters.

Essentially, there was no point of reference for promoters or investors to measure the financial risks or the possibility of success. In other words, there hadn't been a similar show on the national level that had done what I wanted to do with this one. There had never been a play to tour nationally starring six Black, gay male characters as the focus prior to 2002.

Subsequently, I convinced myself that the show wasn't good enough to tour and that I wasn't a gifted writer, rather than consider the possibility that the show was ahead of its time—that perhaps I was a thinker, thought leader, progressive, and dreamer. That I was in fact a visionary. A visionary pioneers ideas, and in most cases the consequence of being forward thinking is being alone in thought, while trying to convince others around you to see what you see.

Consequently, I grew more weary and frustrated from getting knocked down by life. I couldn't seem to fully stand up. I was exhausted from trying. I was tired of needing help, tired of asking for help, and tired of not being in the position to help anyone else in need. I realized later that I was being processed.

The universe, God, knows what each of us needs to prepare ourselves for the next level. Often, relationships represent a major blow that almost paralyzes us emotionally. I believe God uses certain events in our life to prune us for greatness. For me it was financial. I had several cars repossessed, there were threats of eviction, overdrawn bank accounts, and so forth. For others it could be a battle with cancer, the death of a parent or child—it may even come in the form of a divorce. But, on the other side of those circumstances, we're poised to come out renewed, stronger, bolder, more courageous, and more fervent for life.

Thinking back, I just couldn't seem to catch a break. I never seemed to have money for the things I thought were necessary to move my career forward. There was a point at which I wanted to have a website built to sell my greeting cards. Another time, I wanted to hire a publicist, but couldn't because the money simply wasn't there to afford one.

I tried to save money for rainy days, but some way, somehow, that money was always vacuumed away by unforeseen miscellaneous expenses that set me back—new tires for the car, a speeding ticket, you name it. I just couldn't hold on to extra money. Again, I was being processed. I was being stripped. I wasn't sure if I could make it. I wasn't sure if I had it in me to keep going—to keep pushing. I was being tested to see how badly I wanted the dream to manifest. I understand now that when it's truly your passion, and the work is what you are called to do, then you'll never be able to walk away from it.

I've never considered taking my own life no matter how dark or desperate my circumstances became. But I did feel like I existed in a well of sadness that I couldn't escape. I was swaddled in a web of hopelessness, despair, and defeat. I didn't know if I could continue chasing the dream of being a professional writer. Life seemed to be passing me by and I was wasting years in a holding pattern of sorts.

I had become discouraged because I was over-thinking and trying to manipulate the process. Plenty of times I was sidetracked because I was consumed with making things happen and looking for what I thought were the missing pieces to my puzzle.

Now, I understand that the universe, God, was trying to reposition things in my life to move me in a different direction. Sometimes we get set on an idea or a direction and the universe puts roadblocks in place to force us to change course. But, even when it felt like I was off course, I was still very much right where I needed to be. And, no matter how far off course I felt, there were always reminders, hints along the way that I was still moving towards the ultimate dream.

You already have everything that you need to move forward. The universe provides it all. If it's out of your reach, then it isn't necessary for you to grow. If you're unable to acquire it now, in this moment, whatever it is, then you're not at the stage of your career that requires you to have it. There are other things that you can do from where you are. Shift your focus. Focus on those things. Always see the cup as half full—not half empty.

I used to think, "If I could just get in touch with Oprah or Whoopi Goldberg, things would be different." But I realized, instead of trying to reach out to someone who I believed could change my reality by moving my dream forward, what I needed was to network at my level. More importantly, I was responsible for moving my dream forward.

Being ready requires us to possess more than the gift, the talent, the product or the service itself. Readiness isn't limited to the stuff, it isn't restricted to what we do; it bleeds over to our character too. Readiness requires us to possess certain attributes, and sometimes that means pruning us to strip us of certain personality traits to grow us to the next level. Sometimes the key to moving to the next level is about personal growth—changes to your personality or character. Perhaps the talent or business idea is there and ready, but you aren't. I had to learn selflessness, patience and compassion as a part of my process to advance to the next stage in my career. You have to see your growth from a wholistic vantage point. It isn't always about the work you do or the service that you offer. Sometimes there are flaws in your personality that need to be fixed.

Your gift will build your character in ways it hadn't been strengthened before. Your courage will be tested and your will to continue on the road to success will be challenged, because once you decide to pursue your passion and follow the dream, you're also signing up for unforeseen sacrifices, twists, turns and setbacks. And those setbacks will sometimes affect you personally and financially.

So, part of being elevated to the next level has plenty to do with how you handle this part of the process, and how quickly you adapt and grow at each of these stages. I didn't always handle the anguish that came along the journey with the most patience or grace. I often became frustrated and complained when things didn't pan out as quickly or exactly as I wanted them to, which meant my process was prolonged and even more uncomfortable for me. The universe responds in your favor when you accept with ease whatever hardships come your way, and search for the growth lessons rather than complaining and asking why it's happening to you.

At 26 years old, I was skilled enough to write a show that sold out in Atlanta, but I wasn't quite ready for the success of a national tour because my character still had flaws—although, I didn't believe that to be the case back then. I was still learning how to use my gift to benefit others—not just myself. There were also spiritual muscles that needed to be built, then strengthened, and that could only happen after being processed through years of trying and failing with some setbacks along the way. Otherwise, if things had happened for me with very little effort on my part, I would've become bigger than my purpose. I would've believed that I had done it on my own.

I was armed with a college degree, yet living a very precarious financial life. Often, because of my financial circumstances, I battled with depression, in comparison to my friends and other people my age. But then I remembered that I chose to make sacrifices for a bigger reward on the back end of my dream. I sacrificed things that most people couldn't or wouldn't sacrifice for their passion. I was willing to go to whatever extreme the dream took me, even if it meant having cars repossessed, moving back home with family for a period of time, and applying for public assistance. To me, it would all be worth the sacrifice.

While my friends were taking elaborate trips; buying homes, designer clothes; and luxury cars, I was struggling to pay rent on an apartment while trying to hold on to a modest car. I was dreaming of what my life would look like on the other side of the sacrifices I was making. Still, at times it felt pointless having vision without the wherewithal. Thus my dilemma and constant battle was, "Should I give up? Should I continue trusting that the answers, opportunities, and resources will avail themselves to me to succeed?"

As children, passion brews in all of us. Most of us start off with big dreams of becoming a doctor or lawyer. For some, passion gets lost somewhere between childhood and adulthood. Instead of nurturing the idea, parents often ignore a child's dream when it sounds far-fetched or too ambitious. Those children sometimes become adults who have no clue what their purpose in life is because they weren't encouraged, and their talent wasn't honed. If the vision slips away when we're children, it's difficult to get back to it later in life. If we're lucky, we have parents or guardians who expose us to things that summon those gifts to the surface.

Growing up I wanted to be a psychologist, and I shared my dream with my mother. "How many Black psychologists do you know?" she asked. "Black folks don't have no money to see a psychologist. And, White folks certainly aren't paying to see a Black one."

Fortunately, psychology wasn't my passion—it was a career path. But if it was my passion, my mother could have possibly killed that dream in an attempt to protect me from what she believed to be a pointless career choice. That was my first lesson in understanding that sometimes we must keep our thoughts, dreams and ideas to ourselves. Not only because people will have negative thoughts, but also because the people who love us will sometimes project their fears on us. When people know you and love you, they want to protect you. Sometimes this can mean they will try to discourage you from your dream because they don't want to see you get hurt should you stumble and fall.

Some children become adults who lost sight of their passion because they believe that time has run out, and it's too late to follow their dream. Or they simply forego their dream because they have a family to consider first. The world is filled with people with great ideas who lack support, insight, know-how, wisdom and most times the financial resources to see an idea to fruition. I often wonder how positive the world would look if we were all in tuned enough to listen closely to that inner voice as God instructs us through life. What would be possible for each of us if we silenced the voices in the world that fuel doubt? I imagine the disparities in the world would be more balanced.

Perhaps, homelessness or other world issues would be eradicated if we all stood in our purpose. I feel inclined to mention the growing number of mentally ill people who factor into the homeless population. Nevertheless, homelessness exists, in part, because there are people who aren't living out their dream, and I'm not speaking solely of those who make up the homeless population. I'm also referring to those who have ideas about how to cure homelessness but choose to ignore their instincts to pursue their passion because the work feels too difficult.

What if we all uncovered our passions, then shared our gifts with the world? Would there be cures for terminal illnesses if prospective doctors weren't deterred by medical school costs or the number of years required to receive an education? What if underprivileged communities weren't underfunded or underserved, but were given a fair shot at a balanced education with the proper resources? How many of those children would flourish if given a fair chance? Perhaps those schools would produce more scientists. What if a criminal mind was used for good instead of evil? The possibilities are endless.

But it doesn't stop there. Imagine the songs we'll never hear because a gifted singer-songwriter lacks stick-to-itiveness. He loses hope because the countless no's encourage him to quit, so his dream of getting signed to a recording deal gets extinguished. He even resigns from the idea of releasing music independently.

Think of the books that we'll never read because an adept writer cowers from difficulties trying to get her work published or she loses focus because of procrastination. Or what if she simply allows her day job to distract her from writing through the night because she needs her sleep?

What about the movies that we'll never see because a novice filmmaker is overwhelmed with trying to secure funding? Dare to imagine other contributions the world would be deprived of if you allow your passion to be suppressed by fear.

Ask for what you need. In particular, ask the universe to order your steps. When I was uncertain, I prayed. I asked, "Dear God, what are the next best steps for my life?"

Timing is critical for every idea, but your talent or gift can't be measured or limited by time because they're God given, and they can't be bound by time. No one has to believe in your dream except you, because once you believe others will too. Trust your gift. Belief plus action equals results.

We're all on assignment for humanity. Think of it this way, what would the condition of the world be today without the contributions of some of the great people that came before us? What if Mother Theresa had never answered the call to a life of missionary work? And, if Dr. Martin Luther King Jr. didn't dare to dream? The world we know and live in would be tremendously different. The single most important thing for us to do with our time on earth is to pinpoint our purpose. Land on that thing you're supposed to do with your life.

The beginning of the journey offers the most tempestuous moments. It's the period when struggles overshadow the joys and it almost seems to make better sense to let go of the idea rather than press on. But every success starts with a rocky beginning.

Consider the day-to-day obstacles that President Barack Obama faced as a young, underpaid junior senator. He was a father and husband with a mound of student loan debt hovering above his head, while trying to provide for his family and create political change in Chicago. Certainly, he experienced days of disenchantment because of setbacks, and at times felt that he wasn't progressing. But the ultimate prize was the presidency that he secured years later. The end was still the end. It wasn't about each day that was less than productive or the congressional bills that he fought for that died before getting passed by Congress. Those weren't defining moments for him. It was the sum of his efforts that became character builders that prepared him for his role as the President of the United States. That was his process.

Microsoft didn't begin as a household name. Imagine the naysayers, disguised as friends of Microsoft founder Bill Gates, who didn't understand the concept of a personal computer during a time that very few people owned or understood the need for one. Consider the level of frustration he encountered as a thought leader; a visionary. Today, everything is computerized, and most people have a personal computer in their home—many of which are powered by Microsoft software.

Before becoming the philanthropic media giant turned billionaire and network owner, Oprah Winfrey began as a young newscaster. Several years into her career, she was demoted from her position as a news anchor to a local talk show host in Baltimore. What do you imagine she was feeling the day she was demoted? Humiliation? Embarrassment? What if she had never rebounded? Oprah Winfrey is best known for her example of giving, through which she taught us all how to give, and she reminded us to live our best life on purpose. That's how she's changed the world we live in.

I believe our conscience is a direct connection to God and our roadmap through life. He grabs our attention when He needs it—by any means necessary. For me, it's late night, early morning when He nudges me to refocus as things go off kilter or are completely turned upside down in my life.

When it first began to happen, I didn't understand why I was unable to sleep. I'd lie awake tossing and turning as my mind bounced from one thought to another—mostly about my career. There were things that He needed me to know. God wanted my attention. God needed me to hear Him, and the middle of the night was when He got my full attention because I had the fewest distractions.

When I was struggling to produce my stage play, I was awakened one night, and I asked, "Why would You give me this vision to write and produce a play, then put so many obstacles in front of me?"

"Because I knew I could trust you to see it through to the end," He whispered.

It was just that simple.

Not everyone will understand your sacrifice. In fact, most don't understand the sacrifices a dreamer makes for the dream. It takes time and it will cost you time away from friends and family. More than anything, it requires you to spend a great deal of time in solitude, building the dream and your character.

It's a beautiful thing to know your passion and purpose in life, but knowing is only the first step of the journey. Knowing is the precursor to wisdom. Knowing is your first clue to get busy doing the work to bring your vision to fruition.

However, wisdom comes later. After trying, making mistakes, learning from them, stumbling, falling down, skinning your elbows and knees, healing, recovering, getting up, and starting over again and again—you'll finally be primed and ready for the journey to success.

Having a vision is exciting, but it's frustrating too, when it feels unreachable. The vision is the first step to success. Before you can get to the vision you must obtain wisdom, and it takes the right amount of moxie and ego to pursue it fervently. You have to be bold and audacious to chase your dream. Wisdom is the work you'll do honing your craft. This is how you sharpen your skill—you learn through trial and error because you won't have all of the answers when you begin.

Following one's true passion is possibly the most difficult work you'll do in life. You'll know if it's your passion if your desire to respond to the call is greater than your fear of it not working out. You'll know if it's your passion if your desire to respond to the call is greater than your fear of failing in front of the people who know you.

More specifically, your concerns about what people think or say will dwindle. Fear is the reason that so few stay the course. Many veer off course because they worry about what their friends and family will think. People like to see you succeed to have something to aspire to, and someone to tear down.

Ego brought me to this moment. You have to have more than a bit of ego to run to your dream. But ego can help or hurt us if it's not managed, because it can become arrogance. More times than not, ego has helped me. It dared me to believe and dream that I could do and be anything that I set my mind to. Ego is the reason I became a writer. I was courageous enough to believe that there were people who would be interested in reading what I have to say.

Ego gave me the boost of courage that I needed to write and produce my first stage play at 26 years old—not knowing if I'd procure the money to rent the theater or if I'd sell out the show. Nevertheless, I cast the show and rehearsed an ensemble cast five days a week before I even had the money to cover the cost of the production.

Ego gave me the courage to sell everything I owned to move across country to California with a suitcase of clothes and $1,400. I moved to Los Angeles because my instincts directed me, but ego had a lot to do with it, too. I had no idea why my spirit was tugging at me to move to a city where I had no ties; a city that I had only visited twice; a place where, at the time, I only knew two people.

I couldn't find the words or logic to explain to my friends or family why I was selling all my belongings— furniture, shoes, clothes, pots and pans—to relocate across the country, but I knew I had to go. The result of that move was my first book, *Words Never Spoken: A Memoir*. If it wasn't for ego, I wouldn't have the nerve to self-promote, self-publish or sell books across all social media platforms.

In hindsight, my memoir would have never been written had I ignored my instinct to relocate, if I'd allowed a few friends to sway me from trusting my instincts. They feared that I was making the wrong choice for my life. The people who love us will try to dissuade us because they care about us and want what's best for us, but they can't always see our vision. Some things you have to keep to yourself, so the decision is yours and yours alone. It does not belong to the people around you. What could be worse than never trying? You can never fail as long as you're following your dream.

Your gifts are intrinsic—they can't be taught. It's your gift, it's your dream, which means you're in charge of it. You decide where it goes and how it's used because it's your calling. It's your passion, it's your purpose, and it's your responsibility to see it through.

If you find it easier to walk away from what you believe to be your passion, then it isn't passion. When it's your passion, you'll always find yourself drawn to it, even after you've made the decision to quit. True passion doesn't allow us to escape. If it is truly your passion, then you'll never be able to walk away completely. You'll always find yourself doing it unconsciously.

Many times in my career I said I was giving up as a writer because it didn't sustain me financially, but I always found myself writing without thinking. The value of what you do shouldn't be attached to money, because delayed doesn't mean denied, unattainable, impossible or unreachable.

Once you latch on to your dream, keep your hands on the plow, and it will manifest bigger and brighter than you envisioned. There are no shortcuts, but remember the end is still the end despite the detours along the way.

The *no* may never change, but your route around it can. The energy that you put behind your dream continues to move it forward even when your spirit is weary. Every email I sent, every phone call I made, and every meeting that I scheduled counted towards my investment in my dream. Even when the results aren't immediate, it all counts towards your investment in you. Nothing is in vain because the effort and intentions behind your actions are what matter most.

When God blesses you to have it, use it. Keep sewing. You'll end up with a wonderful quilt. The universe rewards effort. God rewards discipline and obedience. Create, then allow your gifts to go wherever they may.

Never stop dreaming. Never stop believing. Never stop wishing. Never stop hoping. Most importantly, never stop praying.

Decide that giving up is not an option. When you're great at what you do, others have no choice but to notice you. Hold on a bit longer. Your turn will come. If you see it, you can have it. Believe it.

Now go. Do. And be.

7 Faith vs. Religion

Separate what you know to be true from what you've been conditioned to believe…

Craig Stewart

We all have the gift of intuitiveness, which is tied to our instincts. Our instincts are designed to guide us on our journey, and through every life decision. But there's an art to really tapping into one's intuition, and more times than not we ignore that internal guide because we get distracted by the voices in the world.

Instincts never lie. We all have them. So, how is it possible to find ourselves in situations or under certain circumstances that aren't best for us? How is it possible that a relationship or business decision can feel so right in the moment, but later we see just how obvious the flaws were? It's simple; we allow the truth to be clouded with what we want it to be instead of seeing it for what it is. We fail to pay close enough attention to the signs, the omens, that tug on our spirit.

My instincts attempted to guide me around a car accident that I found myself involved in many years ago. I chose to silence that little voice that whispered to me to travel the way I always drove home. The consequence of not listening to my instincts was the car accident. It was a seminal moment in my life in which I learned to rely on that inner voice—to really hear that voice and respond accordingly. But, in the instances that I didn't listen to my internal compass, there were always consequences.

Intuition is also that eerie feeling we get just before something tragic or traumatic happens to us or around us. It's those unexplained feelings we have when we simply can't trust a person, but we have no tangible proof for why we can't trust them—we just know we shouldn't.

Intuition is that feeling you get just before the phone rings with someone on the other end calling with bad news, but you felt it even before you picked up the receiver to answer—you knew instinctively that something wasn't right. It's the voice that instructs us to walk away from a relationship because something isn't right. Some people ignore these feelings because they need a reason to explain to themselves, and to those around them, why the relationship ended.

I believe that we can use our instincts to summon someone into our life just by thinking about them. Have you ever thought about someone you hadn't seen or talked to in a long time, only to run into them unexpectedly a short time later in the most random place? Have you ever received a phone call, a text message or an email from someone moments after thinking or speaking about them? You summoned them.

I believe this intuitive nature can be harnessed and applied to every aspect of our life if we trust ourselves enough—if we pay closer attention to every detail of our life. We have the power to will things into existence. It's not magic. It's energy.

Faith is an extension of our intuition, our instincts. Faith is knowing what you know, even when there's no proof. It's that undeniable belief in something or someone when there's no rhyme, reason or tangible evidence that it exists or that you should believe.

African slaves relied on spirituality. Spirituality gave them something to hold onto to survive the tempestuous waters of the middle passage on slave ships. Spirituality strengthened them while they toiled through those cold winter months in corn and cotton fields, and through summer heat across hundreds of years of slavery. In turn, the descendants of those slaves continued a ritual of spiritual practices. But Christianity took a front seat for many slaves and lasted throughout slavery onto the Jim Crow era, and it continues today.

Religion, not to be confused with spirituality or God, has helped and hurt us as a people. I would even venture to say that religion can be tied to all that's right and wrong in the Black community, reaching all the way back to slavery. Religion, like slavery, is a system of control. It's always been steeped in power, control and ownership. Religion has always been a tool that man has used to leverage power in order to maintain control over people, and that truth dates back to slavery.

We're often blinded by religion. As quoted famously by Desmond Tutu, "When the missionaries came to Africa, they had the Bible and we had the land. They said, 'Let us pray.' We closed our eyes. When we opened them, we had the Bible, they had the land."

Historically, religion was used to justify, manage, and control slaves. Religion was the only thing that the colonizers allowed African slaves to have. Everything else was taken away from them—their families, education, their language, and of course their freedom. One of the only freedoms African slaves were allowed was the ability to practice Christianity, and to learn about Jesus through all of the biblical stories that were given to them by the colonizer. Those teachings were intended to brainwash and control them, and us, for generations to come. It worked.

Today, many people of African descent are still enslaved by religion, with the exception of the inquisitive millennial generation who by nature refuse to be fed the same tales that previous generations bought as truth without questioning. That said, most of what you believe to be true about religion was given to you by whoever taught you religion. And it's considered blasphemous to challenge or question things in the Bible, even if it doesn't make sense logically or there are things that we don't understand. We take it all at face value.

My maternal grandmother taught me religion. She taught me how to pray. She was Catholic, but my mother raised me to be Baptist. Nevertheless, when I pray to say my grace, or before bed at night, I always close my prayers by crossing my heart and acknowledging the name of the Father, and of the Son, and of the Holy Spirit.

There are so many rules that have nothing to do with spirituality as much as they do with religion. There are so many things that I question now as a fully formed, critically thinking person that I could never have questioned before. I come from a pretty intact, but dysfunctional family. No one makes it through this life without some sort of emotional trauma. Each of us has our own, some of which is passed down generationally. Other traumas we pick up along our respective journey through life. But we have the power to heal. For me, a lot of my healing rested on religion.

My grandmother believed that it was disrespectful to watch television or to listen to music after we had already said our prayers. That was one rule that made absolutely no sense to me. What if I had said my prayers, but was having trouble sleeping, so I decided to watch television until I drifted off to sleep? Singing at the dinner table was another no no because it was said to be disrespectful to God. Rude? Yes. But, disrespectful to God? I doubt it. I don't believe so. I just don't believe that God is that trivial. I don't believe that He grades us with the same scale that man uses. God is bigger than religion.

I think the vast majority of people are afraid of religion because they feel forced to pretend to be someone they're not. They feel forced to be perfect or rigid. They feel forced to live up to a standard that man put into place, not God. Most religions, in theory, force people to believe that they have to live perfectly in order to be pleasing to God, and certainly to make it through the gates of heaven for eternal life.

More than likely, the religion that you practice today was passed down to you by the people responsible for raising you, unless you converted to another religion at some point. It's customary to adopt the belief system of our family. We're a product of the people who raised us— who they are, what they believe, their values, their priorities, their principles and often their religion.

That isn't to suggest that there aren't people who don't challenge the religion they were raised to believe and practice. Some go on to choose a different religion to practice later in life, or none at all. But generally speaking, religion is passed down generationally.

African slaves were trained and conditioned to fear religion while being encouraged to practice it. However, they were discouraged from ever questioning the Bible stories that were taught to them because the stories were themed in their oppression and inferiority as a people. African slaves were taught that it was God's will for them to be servants.

Religion still has some shackled mentally in ways similar to slavery. Now however, we see Black people using religion to control other Black people, through manipulation of Bible verses that seduce congregants to make sacrificial offerings that are sometimes disguised as a building fund or love offering for the pastor. In exchange, there's a promise that a blessing from God will soon follow.

The church has become a place to hide and judge others. It's a community, in part, that uses the Bible and religion to justify hate, while pretending to be Godly. Religion prohibits many within the church community from thinking progressively—more reason the millennial generation rejects traditional forms of religion. It's in their nature to be more progressive in their thinking, in their beliefs and in their dreams for themselves.

Religion is the excuse some people use to justify hate, discrimination, persecution, and condemnation of groups of people that are different from them, such as gay people—similar to the way that colonizers used religion to justify enslaving Africans. Religion is the reason that most LGBTQ people believe that their sexuality puts them on the wrong side with God. Ultimately, they have difficulty reconciling their spiritual beliefs with their sexuality. Religion is also the reason that some parents disown their children for being LGBTQ. Part of the reason that Donald Trump garnered votes from people that traditionally voted Democrat was that many evangelicals weren't pleased with how inclusive President Barack Obama was with LGBTQ rights.

Religion is the handiwork of man. Spirituality is our relationship with God, while our conscience is our compass to God, and prayer is our source and direct connection to God. Ministers, rabbis, priests and other religious leaders are lauded for their speaking abilities, but their ability to quote religion doesn't always equate to anointing. Some are just well versed in religion, which can be dangerous if their teachings come from a personal place, and not from a spiritual place.

There are parts of the Bible that feel purer than others to me. There are sections of the bible that feel more authentic, as if they come from a place of integrity and honesty with true intention, while other parts feel more calculated, deliberate, outdated and manufactured. Thus, I had to separate what I was taught to believe from what I believe to be true for myself.

Just about every religious community calls for us, the people, to live life according to the rules outlined by their respective religion. Somehow the same standards don't always seem to apply to our spiritual teachers or leaders. Seemingly, the rules and standards are in place for the rest of us to live up to because many of those who hold us accountable to these standards oftentimes do the opposite of what they preach, and fall short in their own life.

There's an unspoken expectation that many followers of religion have of their leaders, and that is to be perfect, maybe even superhuman. And when the leader proves to be human, their reputation is tarnished. It's the reason most congregants are devastated when their spiritual leader is caught in some sort of scandal.

A pastor can fall from grace following a scandal, and his entire congregation might abandon him and the church, as in the case with a number of notable megachurch pastors. The very people who once supported and believed their leader was anointed because he lived his life in ministry, will turn their backs on him because they were foolish enough to believe that if, in fact, he was anointed, he was also Godlike, or infallible at the very least.

There are plenty of contradictions in religion, and it goes without saying that we all have a bit of hypocrisy in us. Anyone who says otherwise isn't being truthful with themselves. That observation stands true even for religious leaders and teachers, although many will pose as perfect when given the chance to pretend. But they, too, are human and aren't infallible. The truth is, many broken men become religious teachers in our communities with hopes of concealing their brokenness from themselves and us, or to share their life experiences.

8 Death

Sometimes the gift is in letting go…

Craig Stewart

I had lunch with a friend today, and while we were chatting, she spotted someone over my shoulder that she knew. He was getting out of a BMW SUV.

"Can I give you a hug?" she called out from our table.

I'm not certain how he replied, but I'm assuming that he welcomed the hug because she stepped away from the table. I turned to look briefly but didn't really pay much attention to the older gentleman because she literally hugged him, and then came right back to the table where we were seated on the patio.

When she returned, she asked if I saw the man that she hugged. Before I could respond one way or the other, she said, "Oh my God. I think I'm gonna cry."

There were tears forming in her eyes. She confessed that the man's ex-wife, whom he divorced some twelve years prior, shot and killed their adult children—a son 25 and a daughter 20—before shooting and killing herself. It was a murder suicide that shook Atlanta's prominent Black medical community.

Immediately I turned around to get a better look at him. He was gone. He had slipped inside a barbershop. My friend said, "No one's seen much of him since this all happened a few weeks ago. I guess he came out to go on with his life."

She was shocked that I hadn't heard about the story which happened a handful of weeks prior, and which made national news headlines. She pulled out her cell phone to show me some of the news articles that were written about the murders. From one of the articles, I found the Instagram page for the surgeon's ex-wife. There were pictures upon pictures of his ex-wife with their daughter in various cities around the world. The last Instagram post was a slideshow of pictures that his ex-wife had posted of herself and their daughter in Italy. She'd posted the pictures on Instagram on the very same day that she took their lives in their Atlanta home while the children were sleeping.

In one of the articles, I read that the doctor's former wife was also a surgeon. I scrolled through her Instagram page searching for clues or signs about why this beautiful woman, who, from the looks of the photos, seemed to adore her children, would shoot them to death in their sleep. I was looking for something that would foreshadow the doom that must have been looming over her life. There wasn't a hint of motivation in any of her pictures.

I wondered if it was to spite her former husband because of some unresolved issue that she never atoned for after their divorce was final. But this couple had been divorced for twelve years. Of course, this means nothing because I've seen people who are still living, but dead on the inside because they couldn't cope after a personal trauma, such as a failed marriage or the death of a loved one. Death isn't just about the physical form leaving earth. Death happens in the spirit too.

Perhaps, this woman's spirit died in that divorce and she never recovered. More importantly, no one recognized that she was no longer herself. There are people whose spirit dies, but they're still living. Their spirit has vacated their body. After compartmentalizing a trauma that they experienced, they're existing with little to no presence of mind. Instead of sitting in the pain, processing it with acceptance, with little to no regret that the trauma occurred in the first place, they feel nothing. Sometimes we put things up on a mental shelf or tuck memories away in the back of a mental drawer with hopes of not ever having to deal with them again.

Perhaps the doctor's ex-wife had an extreme case of undiagnosed mental illness. I wrestled with why because I simply couldn't wrap my brain around the scenario, but my mind wandered back to my friend's doctor—the ex-husband.

I wondered how he managed to go on with his life in a functional way after something so heinous. I mean, he was out getting a haircut when others in similar or less extreme cases of loss or death can't manage to pull themselves out of bed, let alone brush their teeth, get dressed, and leave home for a barber appointment.

I can't say definitively whether or not this speaks to his emotional threshold for pain and grief, or if it simply means that we're all wired differently. Some experience tremendous loss in a tragic way, yet, find a way to continue moving through life. Others collapse in their emotions— never to regain composure after a loved one dies, even in cases of natural causes after living 80 to 90 years. Instead of living they spend the remainder of their life in mourning.

I'm not suggesting that mourning is unnatural, or that there's a specific timeframe during which one should recover from a loss. I'm speaking more specifically about people who experience a death in their life, and never recover enough to continue living their own life. They exist solely on memories that keep them breathing from day to day. Death gives life purpose. When we witness death, it should push us to live more fervently and purposefully.

Dying has always been an aspect of life that's frightened me—how I'll die primarily, followed by when I'll die. One of the many questions that I've asked myself time and time again is whether or not I will accomplish most of the things that I've set out to do before it's my time to pass on.

Aging doesn't scare me—death does. Death separates us. It takes us away from the people we love. It brings an end to lifelong relationships because it decides for us when it's over. Death is final. It pulls families apart.

When my maternal grandmother passed, it left my family divided. The way that we celebrated holidays changed forever. She was the glue that kept us together, but in her absence we separated. All of her children began celebrating holidays with their own children. Holidays were no longer celebrated across families or generations.

I've witnessed the profound affects that death had on a friend of mine who outlived all of his lifelong friends. He was so scarred from loss that he built a wall around his heart and refused to welcome new friends into his life because he was afraid of losing them too.

Death is like music in the sense that it can feel like a time capsule. Music can transport us to a place and time in our life, and death does the same. I'll never forget being a junior in college when Princess Diana was killed in that car crash in Paris. I was with a group of friends when the news flashed across the television screen.

Death should refocus us on our purpose in life, and Princess Diana's death did that for me. So did the death of R&B singer Aaliyah who was killed tragically in a plane crash traveling from the Bahamas to Opa-locka, Florida. I learned of Aaliyah's death from a friend who happened to be visiting me. He's from the Bahamas, but he was living in Atlanta. He was at my place when he received a call from someone back home with the news of the crash. I was in disbelief. Two hours later, CNN and every news outlet were reporting that the plane carrying Aaliyah and her team had crashed.

Years later, I was equally shocked when I heard the news that Whitney Houston died in a hotel bathtub in Beverly Hills. I was living in Los Angeles when it happened. My roommate at the time worked for the hotel and was there when she passed. She called home to say that she wouldn't be home for a few days because there was so much commotion at the hotel. Paparazzi swarmed the property.

My roommate was asked to stay round the clock. Days later, when she finally left work to come home, a tabloid offered her $25,000 to tell them what was going on inside the hotel. There were even radio stations and news outlets from around the world that called the hotel, while broadcasting live, with hopes that an unsuspecting hotel employee would blurt out information about the singer's death. I had passed that hotel countless times before, but after Whitney's death I could never pass it again without thinking about her.

Death is sudden, even when we're on notice to mentally prepare. Still, the moment that life slips away, it feels foreign and unexpected. Death is necessary, but the sadness that results from grief has the potential to swallow us whole if we're not careful.

There are no quick solutions for how to recover after a death because it impacts each of us differently. But I believe the way to honor a life that's been lost is to mourn the loss while remaining steadfast and active in your own life. The way to respect death and the loss of a life is to flourish and thrive in your own. When we allow ourselves to drown in the pain and be overcome by sorrow, it dishonors and tarnishes the life we lost.

We must be patient with the pain that comes from any type of broken heart. After losing a loved one, sit in it and allow it to have its way with you, without losing yourself completely or allowing death to keep you from having a life. Staying in the pain indefinitely doesn't measure your love for the person you lost and moving on with your life doesn't mean that you've forgotten them or that you love them any less. It simply means that you have a life to continue living.

Death humbles us. It makes me uneasy because I don't want to be forgotten. That may sound a bit narcissistic, but it's honest. Death feels final, although most religions suggest some sort of life after death in the spirit form. When I think about my own mortality, I imagine dying well into my nineties from natural causes. Isn't that how most people want to die—in their sleep, naturally?

I've never feared that my life would end violently or tragically, and there's no family history that points to an abridged life. My grandparents on both sides of my family lived well into their eighties or nineties, and since people are living longer now, I suppose I'm in pretty good standing.

I've witnessed friends lose parents, and family friends who journeyed on, but I had never had any close experiences with death that rattled me until my maternal grandmother passed in 2004. Prior to that, I never knew what it was like to lose someone or to be shattered by the death of someone I loved.

My grandmother decided that she was complete. She was done living and was ready to go, but we weren't ready for her to leave. I remember her telling my mom that she was tired. In denial, my mother asked my grandmother rhetorically what she meant, but she knew. She just wasn't ready to hear those words coming from my grandmother, especially if the doctors hadn't forecasted death.

Through my grandmother's death, I learned how selfish we can become when people transition. Not just in the sense of material things, power or money, but in the way that we try to hold onto a loved one even if they're suffering through pain. We even do it with those that have lived long, fruitful lives. It's always too soon for us, but through God's eyes it happens in order.

My grandmother lived to be 96 years old, so she had a full life. I spoke at the funeral and I spoke about the role that she played in shaping my life, the lives of her thirteen children, and all of their children. She had a way of making each of us feel that we were most important.

As I mentioned before, our family dynamic changed when she passed. We weren't as cohesive. We were divided. The breaks between family functions grew. We sometimes go months without coming together—at times skipping holidays together. My grandmother kept us together without trying. Her home was the place that we congregated for everything, and nothing at all.

It's amazing how the ripples from a single life can send vibrations into the world and impact so many others. Perhaps, instinctively we held on to her tighter when she was ready to go because we knew without her that we wouldn't be the same family.

Watching my parents age has become one of my biggest life challenges, and because I don't live in the same state with them, I can see the aging process creeping up on them each time I go home for a visit. My mother began slowing down considerably when she was diagnosed with renal failure and was forced to begin dialysis.

Initially, I was angry with her, because she hadn't prioritized her health. She smoked cigarettes for a good portion of her life, and I remember begging her over the years to quit. My fear was that she wouldn't be around to see me live out my dreams, which was also a point of disappointment for me with my grandmother's death. But I had an even bigger fear that my mom would get cancer.

My anger and disappointment about my mother's health subsided when I accepted that I was powerless over her life and her choices. One New Year's Eve, I scribbled on a sheet of paper all the things that I had to release and leave behind before going into the new year. I folded the paper and tossed it into the fireplace. Burning the paper in the fireplace was symbolic of letting it all go and leaving it behind. To that end, each of us is responsible for ourselves and we can only be held accountable for the life choices that we make for ourselves.

Subsequent to my mother's kidney failure, she experienced a string of complications once she began her weekly dialysis treatments. So much so that I began panicking whenever my aunt Gloria or sister called me. Sometimes the calls were simple updates and other times they represented a big scare. Their phone number would flash on my screen and like clockwork my heart would begin racing. I flew home more times in a matter of months than I had the entire previous year.

I was in the shower one afternoon when I heard my cell phone ringing. The first call came through, and was then followed by a second and third call. The phone seemed to ring nonstop. I was scared and angry at whoever it was calling me back to back. My mind was scattered. I was paranoid. I knew it had to be about my Mom, and if it wasn't, I was going to curse out whoever was calling me nonstop.

I hopped out of the shower without drying off completely. I tracked water all over the bathroom floor onto the carpet in my bedroom trying to find my cellphone. I saw the red missed calls from both my sister and nephew. They'd both called me back to back. This wasn't a coincidence. It was about my mother. I felt it. They had taken turns serving calls back and forth to my phone like a ping pong match.

I called my nephew first, since he and I live in the same state.

"Hey, what's up?" I quizzed.

"My mother just called. She said Gran couldn't breathe. She's on her way to the house," he said.

My nephew began calling my mother Gran when he was a baby. Now his children and the rest of my family call her Gran as well. "Did she call 911?!" I asked.

"I don't know. And, I just tried to call Gran and she's not answering," he said.

"I'll call you back!" I said and hung up the phone.

My heart thumped as I dialed my mother's number. She hadn't picked up when my nephew tried to reach her, but she answered when I called. "Hello," she wheezed.

Her breathing sounded constricted. I could barely make out what she said. It sounded like she was suffocating from an asthma attack.

"What's wrong?" I asked.

"I can't breathe," she wheezed again.

"Call 911!" I shouted.

"I don't need an ambulance. I need my inhaler. It's downstairs," she gasped.

"Ma, you need to call 911! Donnie's on her way," I barked.

I hung up and called my sister to find out how close she was and told her to call 911 because I wasn't too sure if my mother would or could call for herself. I couldn't call because I was in a different state, so the call would have routed to the emergency system in Atlanta, not Baltimore.

My sister was still about 10 mins away.

"Did you call 911?" I asked frantically.

"No, I'm almost there," she said.

"You need to call 911 and have them meet you there. That should've been your first call—not me," I fussed. It wasn't my intention to snap at my sister for not thinking to call 911 because I knew that she was frantic. But in that moment, I couldn't help but snap because of fear.

"Ok, let me call them," she said.

My sister and the ambulance arrived almost simultaneously. The medics gave my mother oxygen, then transported her to the hospital for observation.

Fortunately, it was just another scare, but a very close call that could've turned out very differently. I'm grateful that it wasn't my mother's time to go.

Every relationship has a different expiration date. No relationship is meant to be forever, but every relationship is designed to teach us things. Once we have those lessons, we must let go and move on because the relationship as we knew it dies and the processes of life continues.

Release yourself from regret and live.

9 Trust

Trust is built or broken by consistent behavior...

Craig Stewart

There's a lot to be learned about trust. In order for us to begin the process of trusting something or someone, we must feel confident, sure, and safe. Trust is born out of consistent behavior that's positive, and transparent. If the pattern isn't positive, then trust isn't formed. Doubt forms instead.

Quite often when we think of trust, we think in the context of relationships. But there are degrees of trust. I may trust that you'll never steal from me, but I may not trust that you'll never betray my heart. I may trust that you'll never physically hurt me, but I may not be able to count on you to keep your word or to do the things you say you're going to do. Moreover, it's possible for us to trust someone else's decisions or instincts, but not to trust our own.

Generally speaking, we limit trust to our belief in something, or our reliability in someone. We may relegate trust to relationships, commitment, and love, but trust isn't limited to interpersonal relationships—it's also intrapersonal.

In my twenties, I was fearless and bold, and often threw caution to the wind with respect to taking chances in my career as a writer. But, after a rash of poor financial risks, I was afraid to trust my own instincts and I was unsure of the next best steps for my life.

I became afraid of taking risks because I knew what those risks cost me previously—repossessed cars, overdrawn bank accounts, evictions, bruised pride, and more. It's never easy getting over the sting of financial setbacks and losses. Plus, I had begun to compare myself to others to measure where I was with respect to them, which is a cardinal mistake. Everyone's journey is different, and our life lessons are delivered and packaged uniquely for each of us.

I had become nervous about taking chances in my career because I was getting older and becoming more practical and paranoid. Before, it was nothing for me to pack up everything I owned to move clear across the country from Georgia to California. But now, I questioned decisions that I had made previously and wondered what mental space I had to have been in to do so, and I wondered if I was done making such unforgivable decisions that felt like mistakes at the time.

In some instances, I failed to make a decision. I did nothing when I should've done something. To make no decision is in fact a decision. Thus, I had to regain my own trust and confidence to prove to myself that I could make better life choices. And, I had to realize that the decisions that I had made up to that point were all necessary because the universe always works in our favor to push us to the lessons we require to achieve our highest potential.

Once I released that fear that I spoke about earlier on my flight to Los Angeles, I began trusting myself again. It was a simple shift in mindset and perspective about everything that had happened to me. Regardless of how big or small the issue or circumstance was, I asked the universe, God, what I was supposed to learn from it. Before long, I began to embrace the idea that no matter what happens to me, it's all intended to move me in the direction that I desire in my heart. To this day, I push myself to trust my instincts because we only ignore them when we don't trust them or ourselves to make the right choices.

I had a friend who was behind in all of her bills. She was stuck—so she thought. She believed the answer to her financial problems rested with the men in her life—the ones that she dated and her brother. But they represented only a temporary source. They weren't the answers to her problems. She didn't trust that she would be ok without their help, so instinctively she reached out for help before activating her own power.

I knew the space that she was in all too well. I explained to her that she'd find her way out of that phase of her life once she figured out why she was in the position of need, and what she was to learn while there. But she was more focused on how she could be more creative in how she asked for help rather than focusing on what the circumstance was designed to teach her. I had lived it and survived it to tell her all about it, because the lessons from my process weren't just for me. These lessons were now available for her and anyone that I shared them with.

Nothing great happens inside a comfort zone, so that moment in her life was for the sole purpose of stirring her to action. Her anguish and uncertainty were there to trigger her survival instincts. Instead, at least in the moment that she and I spoke, she felt trapped and unsure of how she would manage. She didn't trust that God would see to it that she would be ok. She didn't believe that He would be there at every impasse, waiting with a solution.

Typically, we fret about things that we can't change, which draws in more confusion, distress and panic. Instead, we should release it all, and surrender to whatever comes our way—even if that means allowing your car to be repossessed, allowing the eviction or home foreclosure process to take place. Don't resist. Release it. Surrender it willingly. Trust that you have it in you to get it all back again, plus more. But even greater than that, think of the goodness that will be generated from what feels like a disaster right now.

Part of the test is getting the lesson as quickly as possible so you can move out of the space you're in. Trust that everything that happens to you is designed to teach you something. Most say they believe this, but they never actually apply it to every aspect in their life, including something as simple as a flat tire that results in you being stranded on the side of a road.

I remember when my Mother was diagnosed with kidney disease. My mother was forced to rely on family more and more once she began her dialysis treatments, and her ability to adjust to relying on us now more than ever proved to be more difficult than the treatments at times.

She was used to coming and going as she pleased. Her frustration was rooted in her inability to serve herself fully.

My mother's renal failure was the result of smoking all of my life and not taking the best care of her health. I believe some of her biggest life lessons were delivered to her through dialysis. It taught her how to ask for help, and how to rely on others.

The quicker that we can unravel the answers to the questions, the faster we can elevate our lives. It's okay to need help and to ask for it, but we are the source; we are the answer to our own needs.

Focus. Get still. Ask for what you need. Trust your life decisions.

10 Integrity

Integrity is a necessity for greatness...

Craig Stewart

Maya Angelou is famous for saying, "When you know better, you do better." But I would argue that we don't always do better simply because we know the best thing to do. Of course, she meant in theory when we know what's right that we should be conscious enough to do what's right. But in order to do the right thing we must vibrate at a higher level to choose what's best and not what's beneficial for us.

In the early 2000s, I had a friend who worked for a semi-luxury men's and women's clothing store, and eventually they began selling home goods as well. The scheme just happened one day. It seemed serendipitous at the time, but thinking back, I believe my friend had been plotting the idea long before he approached me for help to pull it off.

Now, he didn't just come right out and tell me that he wanted us to steal. He called me one afternoon from the store and asked what I was doing. Once he gathered that I was free, he spoke hypothetically, in a joking kind of way, about how easy it would be to steal from the store because the store managers frequently left him unattended on the sales floor. He said, "I could just let somebody walk right out of here if I wanted to, and no one would ever know."

He knew that I'd be intrigued because I often wore their clothes, and I had used his employee discount before to purchase things in the past. He enticed me more by saying that we could make some money too, because he could also pull some items from the sales floor to initiate a fake return, and the money would go to my debit card. We could split it later once the funds cleared my bank account. When he mentioned free money, I was hooked. I told him what I wanted, and he told me to give him a few minutes to pack everything up.

My adrenaline was rushing as I headed to the store. I decided to park on the back side of the mall because the store had a side entrance that was accessible to that parking lot, and that side entrance was open for customers to enter and exit the store. When I walked into the store it was empty, just as he described. There wasn't a single person in the store other than him and me. Nevertheless, we barely spoke. We pretended not to know each other.

I approached the cash register where he was standing, and he retrieved four large shopping bags from the counter behind him. I made two quick trips to my car to place the bags in the trunk and returned to the store so that he could process a return on some other high-ticket items that he had resting on the counter next to the shopping bags. I handed him my debit card, he swiped, the return processed, he handed me a receipt reflecting the amount of the credit, and I left the store. Later that day, he came to my apartment for his things and we gloated about our little caper and agreed to keep it secret.

But that wasn't the only time that we pulled our little scheme. In fact, it became a regular thing. We did it so often that my wardrobe and home furnishings were courtesy of that store. We had everything from flatware and dishware to suede and leather jackets to cashmere throws. Once we had everything that we wanted from the store, our focus became strictly about processing fake returns, so we could get the cash deposits.

Initially, he was modest with the amount of the returns that he would process. But over time, the refunds grew. It all came to an end because he got greedy. He was in a financial bind and desperate for some quick cash, so he processed a refund to his debit card because I was unable to come when he needed me.

Days after the money hit his account, he was called into the manager's office where they confronted him about the return that he'd processed to his bank. He tried to wiggle his way out of it with a poor excuse that he was returning something he'd purchased, and there wasn't a manager around to process the return. They knew he was lying, but they couldn't connect him to all of the refunds to my debit card, so they gave him the option to resign. I'm certain that they wanted him to resign as opposed to terminating him because he would've had the option of drawing unemployment, and they didn't want that fight.

The interesting thing about karma is that it doesn't always strike back right away. Sometimes karma seeks retaliation or revenge years later. I had a friend who used to say, "Karma's a nasty bitch. You could have two dollars to your name, but that bitch will want four and don't care how you get it. She's taking her four 'cause she don't give a damn about you!"

In my first book, I shared a story about a guy that I was involved with who stole all my winter clothes, in the middle of winter, as retaliation because I wasn't interested in a relationship with him. What I didn't consider, at the time that he stole the clothes, was that all of the things that he took from me were things that I had acquired illegally, which meant I was never going to be able to hold on to any of those things long-term because I hadn't gotten them legitimately.

I'd bought most of those things from a booster, a shoplifter friend, who could steal just about anything from the men's department in any store of any mall, including the items draping the store mannequins. When I staged the last production of my play, *A Day in the Life*, in 2007, I hired him to style me for the thirteen shows where I would come on stage to thank the audiences for attending. The only things that my booster needed from me was the name of the store that I wanted things from, a description of the items that I wanted, his payment, and my sizes. Before long, he knew my style and sizes well enough that he no longer had to ask me. He became so good at styling me, he knew my taste well enough to pick out things for me on his shoplifting sprees to the mall without any input from me.

I didn't understand how the things he stole for me were in direct connection with the things I had stolen years before, until I began to understand my chi, my life force, my personal energy and the energy around me. Once I understood those things, I became crystal clear about intentionality. I realized that the stall in my finances and my career were also linked to my less than integral behavior. The only way to turn those things around was to be impeccable in my actions to protect my energy.

I think most of us aspire to be integral, to have a clean heart, to be pure, but I believe we also desire to be deviant at times too. I believe at the core of who we are, we're good, but there's some contradiction, selfishness, narcissism and self-righteousness in all of us. And at times the universe has to remind us individually and globally of our humanity through tragedies such as the terrorist attack of 9/11, Hurricane Katrina, the tsunami in east Asia and Africa, or the massive earthquake in Haiti.

Integrity is kin to truth. Living with integrity isn't always easy because truth isn't always comfortable, but truth requires more than talk. It demands action. I stumbled across inspirational speaker Jeremy Kingsley on YouTube, and I heard him say, "Integrity knows the right thing, says the right thing, and does the right thing, even if no one is watching."

Integrity is consistent. It's being the same with everyone. It's constant. It doesn't waver or change without notice. Integrity is defined as the state of being whole and undivided.

11 Growth

Seeds have but one option once planted, and that is to grow...

Craig Stewart

It takes courage to chase your dreams, to stand in your truth, to fight for what you believe in, to have a difference in opinion, to be knowledgeable, to be educated, to want more out of life, to be successful, to be wise, to be rich, to be exceptional, to be a voice, to be a leader, to be yourself.

I've been described in many ways, one of which is that I'm self-involved. This couldn't be further from the truth. But, often, when people are unable to control you, including trying to monitor what you think, feel or believe, they mislabel you instead. I've had people who don't know me personally, who have never come into direct contact with me, tell other folk, that do know me, that I'm uppity. Or they say that I think I'm better than other people, which has nothing to do with me, but everything to do with them. I've had people who don't know me personally but resented me because I dared to chase my dreams. I've been persecuted because I wasn't deterred by the same things that deterred them.

But let's take a step back for a moment, because another scenario occurs when we begin growing in a different direction from those in our circle. Sometimes they're not envious or jealous at all. Maybe they just became concerned that your growth will force them to do more, and not settle for the low hanging fruit. They can no longer afford to be lazy around you because something was activated in you.

Folks will put out a lie about you to make themselves feel better, and to conceal their own feelings of inferiority, inadequacies, shortcomings and envy, because they feel overshadowed standing next to you. I've heard whispers through the grapevine that I only think about myself, which is another untruth that's emerged because I don't subscribe to certain mores. I believe most people confuse self-involvement with characteristics like confident, focus, and being driven.

I had a conversation with someone recently who told me he felt slighted that I don't openly share with him in the way that he shares with me. He continued by saying that when he lost his job, he expected me to check on him to see if he was ok, or if he needed anything.

First, I explained to him that I'm under no obligation to overshare my life details because he chooses to. I went on to say that just because I count him as a friend that doesn't mean I'm required to include him in every aspect of my personal life—some things are private.

Next, I reminded him of a conversation that he and I had previously in which he volunteered that he had put away money for a rainy day, and he was going to enjoy his time off and travel since he lost his job. More importantly, I told him that friendship isn't one-sided. There were concurrent storms in my personal life while he was going through his storm. I was facing my own battles that he wasn't privy to. But I didn't hold him liable for not calling me just to check in to see if everything was ok in my world.

I don't share everything with everyone. I have a tribe, a small circle of people who I trust to give me direction when I'm lost or feeling uncertain about life. But I've also learned to get still to trust my instincts before I trust someone else's opinion about what's happening in my life.

It's a human instinct to want more, but often the people closest to us feel entitled to what's ours, and may want far beyond what we choose to share with them. There's always a desire for more. We, however, have a responsibility to be true to ourselves first. Then we can serve the community and people around us without feeling like we're being held hostage to what a single person wants or expects from us.

Growth is free thinking. It's liberating to strip free and rid yourself of these ideas that are put upon you by others. I've committed myself to discontinuing this grading system by which my friends and family alike place value on our relationship based on their ability to control how I show up in their life.

I've practically had to re-teach myself most of the social norms that my parents and community instilled in me. I had to learn to be selfish with my personal time and to put myself first, which meant that I had to learn to say no if I chose to. In learning that, I've witnessed other people saying yes, when they really wanted to say no, but they lacked the courage to do so. They fell hostage to what people think. And, because saying no is no longer a challenge for me, I'm often labeled as mean, selfish or self-involved—mostly because I don't feel completely responsible for friends or loved ones. We're all responsible for ourselves. That's not to suggest that I'm all for myself, because I'm aware that no one can make it in this world alone, and we all need help from time to time. I'm suggesting that I get to decide if, when, and how I choose to help. I also get to choose the role I play in someone else's life without feeling burdened to take full responsibility for what's going on. With that said, I no longer feel compelled to subscribe to certain shared rules and ideas of society, just because that's what most people do, or because it's what's expected of me.

Case in point, I don't feel pressured or forced to celebrate the milestones in other people's lives such as birthdays, weddings, or Christmas for that matter. It's interesting to see people who get pulled into exchanging Christmas or birthday gifts because it's supposedly the polite thing to do, instead of simply saying, "I'm not exchanging gifts this year," or "That's not in my budget."

When I was starting out as a young entrepreneur, I wasn't in a position to celebrate anyone's birthdays or exchange gifts for the holidays because I didn't have discretionary money. My gift list was limited to my parents, so I didn't expect gifts from anyone, nor did I feel pressured to give a gift to anyone because they happened to give one to me.

Some of my most difficult moments were saying "no" to my mother. My mother and a handful of my friends used to think that my free time also belonged to them because I wasn't working a traditional 9 to 5 job. That meant that somehow, we were sharing my time. Their thought was, "Well, you don't work. Why can't you help us?" I had to explain to them that although I set my own schedule, I wasn't always free, and even when I was free, that didn't mean I was obligated to run their errands or handle their responsibilities with my time.

I've learned that people will ask the same question, but in a different way, with hopes of getting a different answer from you. But "no" is a complete thought and sentence, and when a person refuses to accept no, they're trying to control you.

To that end, mentally, I know my limits and I'm clear about when I need time to get re-centered because I'm mentally exhausted or drained. It's impossible to get centered if I dole out my time to everyone who tries to visit their problems on me. I'm responsible for protecting my energy and well-being so that I don't overextend myself mentally, physically or emotionally. Only I know my limits. My time belongs to me and I get to decide how it's used.

Similarly, I no longer feel compelled to share, either. Some things are for me only. That doesn't make me selfish. It makes me clear about my boundaries and claiming what's mine. The same concept applies to money and things that belong to me. Often, friends and family will try to guilt us for not filling in the gap when they have a lack of resources in *their* life.

The best analogy I can give is the safety instructions on an airplane. The flight attendant safety instructions are clear that in the event the aircraft begins to lose pressure, you should ensure that your oxygen mask is on first before attempting to help someone else. That message is clear, and it's a metaphor for life. Take care of yourself first. But, that kind of self-care requires growth—personal growth.

That time in my life was especially uncomfortable for me because I had no way of knowing when the friendships I lost would be recycled and replaced with healthier and more meaningful ones. I had some dying to do to find me again. God was trying to restore all that I had lost after pruning me because I had gotten distracted on my life journey trying to find success and love. Instead, I found myself imbalanced and disenchanted. I was running on empty, and at full throttle.

I found that many of the choices I had made for my life weren't my own. Many of the decisions that I thought I had made for myself were decided for me by the voices around me. Those voices belonged to my mother and a handful of friends. I had even been influenced by social media.

Even as independent thinkers and thought leaders, we're influenced by the world around us more than we may know. Consider the life choices that you've made based on the opinions of your friends or family, whether you're trying to impress or appease them. I had to stop being concerned with what people thought about me, about my journey, and focus on what I knew to be true about myself. I had to shut off the noise, the voices in the world, the voices in my head, and the voices in my life, to hear the voice of God.

I found myself at a crossroads. I was feeling unfulfilled. I knew what I wanted and what my soul was calling me to do. I wanted to write and produce projects that would provoke people to think differently—on a higher level. I wanted to inspire people, but also to challenge their deepest and strongest beliefs about life and the world around them. The one thing that was holding me back was what people thought about my journey as a struggling writer and artist.

I didn't experience a shift in my writing career until my perspective changed, which occurred after a conversation I had with a friend of a friend. We became accountability partners of sorts. We agreed to stay in touch by phone or text once a month to check in with each other. Our plan was to make sure we each were setting goals and meeting deadlines for the things we said we wanted to do.

I texted him one afternoon because I needed a push. I was feeling unproductive and stagnant. Our text exchange started off like normal. I asked how things were with him, and he did the same. "Things are ok. I'm still grinding. Tryna make shit happen," I texted.

I had no way of expecting what was coming next.

"Actually, try changing your vocabulary. Grind really has a negative vibe about it. It evokes a feeling of struggle or working against something—force. It's definitely a journey, as corny as it may sound. But journey is more encouraging because it promises a definite arrival to your desired destination. Do this for me, first thing each morning, write a list of everything that went well the day before—every little thing to every big thing that worked in your favor. Write it on a sticky note so you can take it with you throughout the day. Each day add an additional sticky note to the one in your pocket. Do this for a full week. When you start to get depressed or discouraged, take the notes out and read them out loud quietly. It's important that you hear your voice saying it to yourself. By the end of the week, tell me how many sticky notes you end up with. Don't overthink it; just do it and be honest," he replied.

My life changed after that day. One of the first goals I set and brought to fruition was my podcast, *So Much to Say*.

Finding balance between gratitude and wanting more can be tricky. It's that sweet spot between trusting the process by releasing the reins of life to allow things to settle on their own and reaching out to touch something beyond your wildest dream. Perseverance is doing everything you can when you're able to push forward and get through the murky points of life. Yet, you have to understand when to release the reins a bit.

It's a long journey from there to here—from the place where you started to the place you envision for yourself. Growth is reaching beyond what's comfortable, what's given to us, for more.

At the beginning of any journey, there's a point along the way that you'll start to question whether the future will ever manifest as you see it in your mind, and the same holds true for introspective growth. In fact, you're wiggling and squirming because you're uncomfortable with the space you're in, and you're sharing your discomfort with anyone who will listen because you've exhausted yourself from praying, meditating, or searching for answers that will help you move along swiftly to the finish line.

I'm of the belief that for as long as we're living and breathing there's always room to grow and build upon the life lessons we've learned.

Every artist, every dreamer and every entrepreneur feels overlooked at one point or another. I've seen artists and entrepreneurs who developed huge egos because they felt they should've made it long before they actually did. Thus, some became resentful and egotistical. Moreover, some refused to reach back to pull anyone else along out of bitterness. But I resolved on my journey that I wouldn't become that kind of artist.

In hindsight, I'm grateful and appreciative of the slow burn I experienced because I would have been overcome by lightning speed success. I believe I would have become bigger than my purpose. Ego would have overtaken me, and I would have forgotten God's purpose for my work and my life. But I also needed to be processed in other areas. There were inherent qualities that needed to be strengthened in me, such as my level of patience and compassion for others. The only way for me to achieve that was through the spiritual growth that came with the obstacles I faced.

The universe has a wonderful way of working hardships into our journey and redirecting us from what appears to be a dead end onto something greater. Growth requires you to trust that everything will work out in the end.

There will always be hurdles as well as other significant life changes that seemingly impede progress. Your passion and desire to grow will be tested at every growth stage to build character and to challenge you to fight.

There's a middle ground between surrendering to the universe and God's will, without becoming complacent. It's easy to become lax, then kick back because you tell yourself that everything will happen in divine time, when it's supposed to. So you never self-motivate.

Get still and listen. Your growth is your responsibility. Growth is critical to you. Lessons are hard. Growth is harder. Grow anyway. One day soon it'll all make sense to you.

ABOUT THE AUTHOR

Stewart attended Hampton University, and graduated with a degree in liberal arts. Following graduation, he relocated to Atlanta where he wrote and produced a stage production entitled "A Day in the Life" that played before a sold-out audience. In 2012, he released his first book Words Never Spoken, a memoir, and in 2015 it was followed by the sequel One Thing for Certain, Two Things for Sure, a memoir continued. His third release So Much To Say, a book of Quotes was released in 2017—all of which carry 5-star rating on Amazon.

Stewart is also the founder of Say it in a Card greeting card company, and host of So Much to say Podcast, which premiered in May 2017. The podcast is heard in 60 countries via Apple, Spotify, YouTube, Soundcloud, Google Play, **Radio.com**, Stitcher and Tune in with a listenership of 86-thousand to date and a combined 40-thousand followers across all social media platforms.

So Much To Say Podcast was born out of a need to build dialogue around subjects that are sensitive, but important to the LGBTQ and Black communities. The conversations center on socially relevant topics hence "TheWriter's" opening catch phrase, "Good day thinkers, thought leaders, progressives and dreamers I'm CraigTheWriterStewart and this is So Much To Say. These are my thoughts, in my voice, on Black sh★t, White sh★t, Gay sh★t and everything in between!"

No topic is left untouched because the intention is to reach, teach and heal while bridging the gap between communities: Black and White People; Gay and Straight men; HIV positive and HIV negative people; Gay and Trans people etc. Some of the shows over the course of the past two years include, "Would You Date Someone HIV Positive or Not," "How Religion Has Helped and Hurt Us As A People," "He Was Born She," and "Man vs. Man – Domestic Violence in Gay Relationships."